ROUTLEDGE LIBRARY EDITIONS:
ORGANIZATIONS: THEORY & BEHAVIOUR

COMPANY ORGANIZATION

T0295596

COMPANY ORGANIZATION
Theory and Practice

M. C. BARNES, A. H. FOGG, C. N. STEPHENS
AND L. G. TITMAN

Volume 1

Routledge
Taylor & Francis Group
LONDON AND NEW YORK

First published in 1970

This edition first published in 2013
by Routledge
2 Park Square, Milton Park, Abingdon, Oxfordshire OX14 4RN

Simultaneously published in the USA and Canada
by Routledge
711 Third Avenue, New York, NY 10017, USA

First issued in paperback 2016

Routledge is an imprint of the Taylor & Francis Group, an informa business

© 1970 George Allen and Unwin

British Library Cataloguing in Publication Data
A catalogue record for this book is available from the British Library

ISBN: 978-0-415-65793-8 (Set)
ISBN: 978-0-415-82311-1 (Volume 1)
ISBN 13: 978-1-138-97130-1 (pbk)
ISBN 13: 978-0-415-82311-1 (hbk)

Publisher's Note
The publisher has gone to great lengths to ensure the quality of this reprint but points out that some imperfections in the original copies may be apparent.

Disclaimer
The publisher has made every effort to trace copyright holders and would welcome correspondence from those they have been unable to trace.

COMPANY
ORGANIZATION
Theory and Practice

PA MANAGEMENT CONSULTANTS LTD

Written by M. C. BARNES, A. H. FOGG, C. N. STEPHENS, L. G. TITMAN

London
GEORGE ALLEN AND UNWIN LTD
RUSKIN HOUSE   MUSEUM STREET

FIRST PUBLISHED IN 1970
Second Impression 1970

© *George Allen and Unwin* 1970
ISBN 0 04 658031 x

PRINTED IN GREAT BRITAIN
in 11 *on* 13 *pt. Times*
BY COMPTON PRINTING LTD
LONDON & AYLESBURY

Preface

The equipment and machinery used in factories and offices have
changed out of all recognition during the course of this century.
Changed too are the actions, attitudes and theories of
management. This book is about that part of management known
as Organization Structure, showing how ideas have changed
and the position that has now been reached.

This book is intended to be of use to managers and to
students of management. It was written by members of
PA Management Consultants Ltd, and includes material used
in the training of their newly-recruited staff.

London, 1969

Contents

CONTENTS

Chapter 1

An Introduction

'And Moses chose able men out of all Israel, and made them heads over the people, rulers of thousands, rulers of hundreds, rulers of fifties, and rulers of tens.' (Exodus 18.)

When Moses appointed rulers over the people of Israel, he was involved in the problems of organization structure. This is one of the earliest surviving records of anyone tackling an organization problem, though it is certain that the problems existed and were tackled long before Moses met them. As an example, we know that the Court and Government of the Pharaohs were very complex and highly structured, whilst the many relics of Egyptian civilization suggest a society of powerful officials, detailed regulations and specific responsibilities.

What was the problem which Moses faced, and which caused him to appoint rulers? It was simply a problem of overwork and the need to delegate. In the Book of Exodus we read that Moses sat from morning to evening judging the people, and that despite the long hours he worked there was always a crowd of people waiting to be judged. Jethro, who was Moses' father-in-law, was blunt – 'Thou wilt surely wear away, both thou, and this people that is with thee: for this thing is too heavy for thee: thou are not able to perform it thyself alone.' Jethro's diagnosis was correct, and clearly sets out what most managers discover early in their careers – a man cannot do everything himself, and must delegate, both for his own sake and for the sake of those he manages. This is a problem which every manager encounters and which has not changed or altered in any way from the time of Moses to the present day. Nor is there any likelihood that it will ever alter.

If then the problem never changes, is it not possible that the solution too is immutable? Was Moses' action – based on Jethro's advice – a

13

unique or a universal solution, which is valid today? Could the modern student of management join the old-time revival meeting and sing 'It was good enough for Moses, so it's good enough for me'?

To test this possibility, we must analyse carefully just what Moses really did; we must try to work out why he shaped his solution as he did; we must also test and analyse some of the things which apparently he did not do, and deduce if possible why they were not done. Once this analysis is complete, then we must try to apply his methods to our circumstances, whether these be in Industry or Commerce, in Government or Institutions.

An important point of analysis is to examine the source of Moses' authority. Who gave him the authority to appoint the rulers of the people? For that matter, where did he gain his own authority over the people? These are important questions, because unless we know the nature of the authority, it is likely to cause difficulty when delegated. If the source and nature of authority are unclear then the authority may be questioned – 'What right have you to order me about?' etc. Fortunately the source of Moses' authority is quite clear: God chose him. Now this was simple, clear, straightforward and in the circumstances of the time an unquestionable authority. But it is of little relevance in the twentieth century. The heads of some religious groups may still be chosen by God, but the Pope is chosen by the Cardinals in conclave, and the Archbishop of Canterbury by the Prime Minister. The heads of industry and commerce are certainly not chosen by God. What then is the source of their authority?

Sometimes authority derives from rank. In the Armed Services, in the event of uncertainty at any time or in any place, authority rests with the senior officer present. A Major is superior to a Captain: and between two Majors, the one promoted first is the senior. Every officer is 'labelled' by his date of promotion, and the authority rests, by Queen's Regulation, on the most senior. Authority by rank is unambiguous, though it does not always produce the best man for each job. Moreover, it rarely works outside the Armed Services, the Police, the Fire Services and similar organizations. Some firms have created badges of rank to be worn by Sergeant Foremen, etc., but it is so uncommon that it cannot provide a general solution.

Authority may derive from position. The Station-Master at Euston is appointed to a position, which endows him with authority. Perhaps the clearest case is found at sea. The master of a vessel has certain powers – very great powers – whether he is worthy of them or not. In the Royal Navy the Commanding Officer of a ship has great and un-questioned authority derived from his position, whether he is a Mid-shipman in command of a launch or a Captain of an aircraft-carrier. Such authority is common in industry or commerce: men are appointed as managers of branches and divisions, etc. But is this the only source and is it the best one? And while this might meet the case of the middle manager, it may not cope with the more senior manager. From where does the Managing Director derive this authority and how does he exercise it?

Moses, perhaps, was grateful that his case was clear-cut. God chose him and sent him to the people of Israel and to deal with any doubters provided him with impressive signs.

Another important point of analysis concerns the numbers of men controlled by each of the 'rulers' appointed by Moses – their Span of Control. One presumes, for lack of any statement to the contrary, that the rulers of tens reported to the rulers of fifties – five junior rulers to each more senior one. But why five? Couldn't some of the more able senior rulers have coped with six, or seven or even more junior ones? And are there any circumstances under which four junior rulers would have been correct? For that matter, why were they rulers of tens? Because the men had ten fingers? But commonly the most junior managers in industry have thirty to forty people to 'rule'. It is at once obvious that Moses' solution does not provide clear guidance at the lower levels. What does he have to offer higher up in the organization? The rulers of hundreds, apparently, have only two rulers of fifties reporting to each of them. What on earth did they do all the time? On the other hand, the rulers of thousands, apparently, each had ten rulers of hundreds reporting to them. Why is there such a huge difference in work load between the rulers of thousands and the rulers of hundreds? Why are there no rulers of five-hundreds analogous to the rulers of fifties? Has something been lost in the translation: did Moses have good reasons for these differences, and if so what were they?

Moses may have been right over these apparently irreconcilable decisions about numbers. In fact he was following the advice of a consultant: in this case his father-in-law, Jethro, who stated, 'I will give thee counsel.' But we have no idea why Jethro prescribed the

15

numbers he did, and his solution is of no real value as a guide to anyone faced with modern organizational problems. Being good enough for Moses just isn't good enough for us.

As to the types of men that Moses made into rulers, all that we learn from the Book of Exodus is that they were 'able men, such as fear God, men of truth, hating covetousness'. As a man-specification this is less than wholly explicit, though there is no ambiguity over men who fear God and men of truth. But 'able' at what? Were they able planners to guide the people of Israel in the wilderness, or were they physically courageous to lead the people through dangers? These questions are not answered, so there is no guidance here for modern organization problems.

Another unresolved problem is whether these able men were all able at the same thing, or whether some of them specialized in various activities. It is a reasonable assumption that the people included priests, transport specialists, catering specialists, and custodians of the flocks and herds which they took. It is at least questionable whether all these specialists should have been organized in the same way, or whether different arrangements would have been appropriate. For example, each ruler of ten might have had his own priest and his own shepherd; or as one alternative, the priest might have been attached to the rulers of thousands and the shepherds to the rulers of hundreds. Exodus provides no guidance at all on this point, but it is an important one for anyone dealing with changes in an organization structure. In modern industry there are invariably specialists, except in the smallest firms. It is common to find a division into Sales, Production, and Accounting functions, with lesser functions such as maintenance, personnel and management services. At various times, different solutions have been applied to this problem, which may be called that of 'the generalist versus the specialist'.

It is an old and untrue joke that, if one goes to a particular medical specialist, one turns out to be suffering from his speciality. But it is perfectly true that a firm which set up a legal division to handle legal affairs found that it became involved in three times as much litigation as previously. On the other hand, if all the specialists are subordinate to the generalists, then experience has shown that the latter are unlikely to make the best use of the specialist talent.

There is one last point on which Exodus gives us a tantalizing

16

glimpse of something we would really like to know about, as students of organization. We would like to know exactly what each level of ruler was able to deal with, and what he had to pass up to higher authority. There is even some ambiguity in the glimpse, for Jethro's advice to Moses was that 'every great matter they shall bring unto thee, but every small matter they shall judge', whereas Moses' decision was such that 'the hard cases they brought unto Moses, but every small matter they judged themselves'. What is the difference between 'great' and 'hard'? Does the distinction lie in the amount which is at stake in the decision, or is it in the intrinsic difficulty of the decision? This separation of decisions, into those which are routine and trivial as compared with the unusual and significant, is the purpose of the whole exercise which began when Moses was overworked.

Our exploration of the Book of Exodus has gone far enough. Moses' problem is our problem – that of delegation. But his solution is of little, if any, value to us. The student of management must turn therefore to the textbooks on the subject of organization structure. He will want to know what factors determine which of the basic structures to use in a particular case, or whether to resort to one of the other structures which are sometimes recommended. He will want to know how to bring into consideration the size of the company, the markets in which it is selling, the range and type of technologies employed. He will want to take account of all these factors, and also of the needs and abilities of the people involved.

For these reasons this book is divided into four main parts. Part A covers the history of the subject and describes the main approaches to it – including the 'classical' approach, the 'human relations' approach, and the 'systems' approach. In Part B we examine the main concepts upon which the various theories have been built. In Part C we discuss the individuals and their effect on organizations. Finally, in Part D some guide lines are set out to be followed in practical work on organization structure. The two appendices include a glossary and a bibliography.

Work with organization structures offers the stimulus of intellectual challenge. Diagnosis has all the excitement of an exercise in deduction. Prescription demands all the creative skills of the practitioner, who must continually educate himself to gain in competence. It is hoped that the remaining chapters of this book will give him a good start.

17

PART A

History

Every successful expedition starts with a survey of the terrain. Information is gathered from maps, photographs, previous expeditions and so on. A preliminary survey of the ground to be covered will also guide the reader through this study of organization theory and practice.

In Chapter 2 we consider three viewpoints on organization. One approach considers an organization as a machine whose aim is to function perfectly. A second approach argues against this, claiming that organizations are composed of people and people do not behave like parts in a machine. The third approach considers the organization in the light of its similarity to biological and other systems: a phenomenon which is constantly adapting, reshaping and wholly dependent on its environment.

Chapters 3 and 4 go behind these viewpoints to the men and women whose intellect, experience and writings have produced them. This review of others' work will serve to raise many of the problems which will be discussed in later chapters and to illustrate the historical background of our subject.

Chapter 2

Approaches to Organization

No man possesses an unlimited capacity for work. Physique, brain-power, training, aptitude, time, place and many other factors restrict human activity. If a man owns a business, the limits on his capacity for work sooner or later force him to seek and obtain assistance from others. He may find that he simply cannot cope with the volume of work. He may require the services of a lawyer or an accountant, or some other specialist assistance; he may be tired of trying to be 'in two places at once'. Whatever the problem, if he obtains the assistance that he needs, he must decide how the work is to be allocated and he must pass down to others part of the responsibility for running the business.

Let us assume that this man is in business because it is his living, and as such the business must make a certain profit. However inadequate and vague a statement, this is the objective of his business and the yardstick by which he will measure his success.

While he alone managed the business, he had, as far as it is possible, full control over his success. If he failed to make the necessary profit, he had only himself to blame. Now that he employs the services of others, part of his control over the fate of the business falls to the others involved in its management. The owner's position becomes more complex. Now he has not only to discipline himself to achieve his objectives, he must also see that his employees co-operate in a way which will contribute to the success of the business. He must co-ordinate their activities.

In this description of the change from a business managed solely by its owner to a business in which others share in the task of management, we have seen the basic elements of organization. We can now define organization as: 'the *division* of *work* among people whose efforts must be *co-ordinated* to achieve specific *objectives*'.

21

The word 'objectives' is the last in our definition, but objectives should be the first consideration in organization planning. Some modern writers have emphasized this by showing that an organization is a type of 'open system'. For survival and growth, an *open* system must be constantly interacting with its environment; input is received from the environment and output disposed of to the environment. The organization, as an open system, must constantly adapt to changes in the environment.

The open system approach to organization emphasizes, therefore, the need to define objectives in relation to the environment. It is the satisfaction that the environment gets from the output of the business that will make available the input, which is essential for survival and growth. The statement of objectives, therefore, does not merely provide a basis for the division of labour, but rather it should be a creed for survival and growth. When Henry Ford said that the customer can have any colour of car 'as long as it is black', he implied that the organization can be independent. On the contrary, an organization is wholly dependent on its environment, and objectives should be drawn up with an awareness of this dependence.

The objectives of a business determine the work to be done. The type of work will vary from level to level in the organization. In our definition, therefore, the word 'work' must be taken to include physical labour, mental activity, and decisions. As we have shown, when the work becomes too great in volume, too varied in character or too dispersed for one manager to handle, it must be divided.

Division of the work load solves the problem of one man's inability to cope, but it creates the problem of co-ordinating the activities of the people among whom the work is divided, so that the objectives are still achieved. A man can co-ordinate the movements of his hands, but how often we hear complaints in companies that 'right hands' do not know what 'left hands' are doing. To avoid duplication, omission and general confusion, activities must be co-ordinated.

'Organization' we said 'is the division of work'. But how do we divide up the work? What are the criteria for deciding that manager A is responsible for this part of the work and manager B that part? What are the main factors to be considered in such decisions? The nature of the work? The personnel available? Efficiency? An unequivocal answer to these questions would solve many organizational problems. As a start, we will consider three approaches to organization which can be distinguished in the work of organization theorists: the Classical approach, the Human Relations approach and the Systems approach.

The Classical Approach to Organization

The Classical approach is founded on what is often called 'Machine Theory'. The organization is viewed as a machine, which is built according to a plan with a rigid specification. The statement of Henry Ford, quoted earlier, typifies the underlying philosophy of much of the Classical approach. Others recommend that a structure should be designed 'in a cold-blooded, detached spirit',[1] as if one were preparing an engineering drawing. Just as the specification is clear-cut and rigid, so the resulting organization has clearly prescribed divisions of responsibility. It becomes static and inflexible. Its strength is thought to lie in its ability to resist, rather than adapt to, internal and external pressures.

It is a short step from considering an organization as a machine, to thinking that organization planning can be condensed into the question: 'Which division of work gives greatest efficiency?' The technique of value analysis shows the savings that can be achieved by reducing the costs of an item while still allowing it to perform the same functions. The same idea is inherent in the Classical approach to organization. First consideration is given to finding the form of organization which will provide the most efficient use of inputs, while maintaining the same output. The search is a useful one, but, as the sole criterion for the division of work, this type of efficiency is inadequate. It may also be self-defeating, since many of the accepted methods of obtaining efficiency have led to inefficiency, when installed against the background of an inadequate concept of organization such as Machine Theory. We shall return to this point when discussing the other approaches to organization.

It would be unwise, however, to reject the Classical approach as totally lacking in validity. The desire for efficiency must affect decisions on organization structure. Also many large and successful companies were nurtured on the principles evolved by the Classical approach, just

[1] L. F. Urwick, *Elements of Administration*, p. 35.

23

as many companies are still organized along Classical lines. Furthermore, out of this approach have developed many concepts which only recently were questioned. And even now, we might hesitate to criticize these concepts, if we were not aware of faults in the general approach that bred them.

Although these concepts will be the subject of detailed discussion at later stages, it will be useful at this point to outline the major implications of the Classical approach, especially since the other approaches we are to consider contain direct contradictions of some of these implications.

A central theme of Machine Theory is the concept of the *specialization of tasks*. Efficiency is attained by the subdivision of operations into their elements. The elements can be taught more quickly, and a high level of performance can be reached more easily. The arguments to support this idea are strong; and if we were to concede that this type of efficiency were the sole or, at least, the main criterion for organizational success, there would be no doubt that specialization of tasks would figure prominently in all theories about organization.

Through specialization, performance not only reaches higher levels but becomes *standardized*. One of the tools of the Classical school was time and motion study and with this tool it is easy to create the idea of the 'one best way to . . . '. This idea may be acceptable at the operator level of tasks, but it must surely find resistance in the fields of research, design and management.

Where standardization of tasks is not possible, *uniformity of practices* supplies the answer. Company-wide practice is specified in such areas as union negotiation, wage structures, and outside contacts.

Both standardization of performance and uniformity of practice presuppose some form of central direction. The idea of central direction is embodied in the two Classical concepts of *unity of command* and *centralization of decision-making*. Specialization brings both a greater efficiency and a greater need for co-ordination. Decisions must be centralized in one command, if company-wide co-ordination is to be maintained. There must be man-to-man responsibility and no supervisor should be asked to control the work of more men than he can effectively supervise. The strength of the organization lies in its clarity, lack of ambiguity and rigidity.

Machine Theory still has a large following, especially among companies engaged in mass production and companies that are 'production oriented'.

Many of the ideas conceived by the Classical approach still recommend themselves when placed against the background of a more adequate concept of organization than the 'machine' concept.

The Human Relations Approach to Organization

The Classical approach to organization not only makes full use of standardization and uniformity within organizations, it also implies a standard formula for building an organization structure. Doubts must have been raised when some companies who applied the formula encountered problems.

One reason for doubt is obvious. The 'machine' concept of organization presupposes the availability of material. When we design a machine we know that we will, without too much difficulty, be able to obtain the metals, plastics, etc., that our design specifies. The materials of the organizational machine, however, include people and although we can specify and hope to obtain people of certain physical dimensions, it would be unwise to think that we could requisition a complete human being who would function exactly according to our specification, as we would expect a piece of metal to do in a machine.

The Human Relations approach emphasizes the need to take full account of people when designing an organization structure. The behaviour of people in organizations is the main object of study; and as a result of this study, psychologists and sociologists hope to prescribe the conditions under which people are more likely to co-operate in achieving the objectives of the organization.

The realization that the individual brings his own needs and values to the organization is the starting point of the Human Relations approach. The specific needs of individuals are uniform only in their diversity. They can, however, be categorized as follows: 'physical needs, security, self-actualization'.[1] (Self-actualization is a phrase which means self-fulfilment, the full achievement of a person's real potential.) The order of these categories is significant; according to the Human Relations approach, people try to satisfy their needs in this order of priority. The more our needs for physical well-being and security are

[1] C. Argyris, *Integrating the Individual and the Organization.*

25

satisfied, the more we feel the need to 'actualize' our full potential. The Classical approach tends only to recognize the needs of lower priority – financial incentives, appeals to physical and, on occasions, security needs. The need for self-actualization is, however, frustrated by standards, uniformity, specialization and over-definition.

Since the central theme of the Human Relations approach is the diversity of human motives and behaviour, we cannot expect from it a direct and explicit statement of the basis for organization planning. To a large extent, the psychologists and sociologists have merely criticized the lack of concern shown by earlier writers for the people who are being organized. The Human Relations approach is an attitude rather than a set of principles of organization, a warning that people are not machines and cannot be treated as such. It is argued, however, that co-ordination is impossible unless people are willing to co-operate. In view of this we can say that the needs and values of people must be taken into account and integrated with the needs and values prescribed by the objectives of the organization.

The Systems Approach to Organization

Machine Theory concerned itself mainly with the production process defined, in its broadest sense, as the process for converting inputs of money, materials and labour, into outputs of goods or services. The Systems approach emphasizes the inadequacy of this as the basis of a theory of organization. An organization is not a closed system whose interaction with the environment is stable, and, therefore, requires little or no attention. It is an open system, and therefore includes, as well as a production process, other processes which are essential for it to maintain its existence, support its functions and adapt to its environment. To this extent an organization is similar to other open systems, such as the human brain. But, unlike the human brain, an organization is 'a structuring of events or happenings rather than physical parts and it therefore has no structure apart from its functioning'.[1] The contrast with the Classical approach is obvious.

What other features do organizations have in common with other open systems? Most important is the principle of *feedback*. Feedback consists of information not only about the performance of the system,

[1] Katz and Kahn, *The Social Psychology of Organizations*.

but also about the environment and the effect of the system's products on the environment. Feedback is essential for survival. It is pointless to manufacture products which no one wants. The receipt of feedback enables the organization to maintain a steady state or *homeostasis*. This is not the static, rigid balance of closed systems but a dynamic steadiness in which the forces of differentiation, elaboration, growth and survival are constantly at work. There is no 'one best way' to achieve homeostasis. The principle of *equifinality* states that a system can reach the same conclusion from different starting points and by different routes; a brand can become brand leader by enlarging the market or by gaining a competitor's sales. This too can be seen as a direct criticism of the Classical approach.

How does the Systems approach assist in organization planning? What bases does it suggest for the grouping of activities and the assignment of responsibilities? If we accept that the purpose of an organization structure is to assist in the achievement of company objectives, then we must study not only the company itself but those parts of the environment that affect the achievement of objectives. We will see that the decisions that the enterprise has to make to achieve objectives will highlight certain functions in the enterprise. For example, an enterprise with an objective of growth may find, on examining its existing markets, that they will not allow growth. Such a circumstance would throw major emphasis on the need to differentiate and exploit a new market. In this case, the closed system approach may have resulted in an expanded sales programme in existing markets, which would have proved in vain.

The open system approach leads to a strategy which is more realistic and likely to be more successful, since it takes account not only of what the enterprise can do but also of the effects of certain actions on the environment.

The Systems approach, therefore, isolates certain important functions; the functions themselves are important because they are concerned in those decisions which contribute most directly to the achievement of objectives. The key activity of the approach is, therefore, the identification of the main decision areas. Then the organization should be designed to facilitate decision-making. But decision-making itself depends on the principle of feedback and feedback presupposes communication channels. In short, given certain objectives, the decisions

27

to be made to achieve those objectives and the communication channels necessary for making those decisions should determine the organization structure.

The three approaches to organization suggest different areas in which the search for criteria for dividing work will find most success. These approaches are difficult to integrate completely. However, they contain a number of basic proposals which most managers would accept. We can summarize these as follows:

To achieve certain objectives, a company has to perform a certain amount and type of 'work'. The division of this work among the employees of the company should take into account
(a) the exact nature and amount of work,
(b) the needs, values and capacities of the employees, and
(c) the decisions to be made and the communication channels necessary to enable the employees to make the decisions.

Even these bases will lead to contradictory solutions and we are still left with the question: which is most important? Even so, the realization that all these factors have some importance, if not equal importance, will contribute to the planning of a more effective organization structure.

Summary

Organization is defined as the division of work among people whose efforts must be co-ordinated to achieve specific objectives.

We can distinguish three approaches to the study of organization. The Classical approach tends to regard organization as a closed system, a machine whose internal efficiency is of prime importance. The basis for dividing the work to be done to achieve objectives is the nature of the work itself.

The Human Relations approach claims that problems of co-ordination in organizations result from blindness to the needs and values of the people who comprise the organization. The division of work should be such as is most likely to evoke a willingness to co-operate.

The Systems approach looks at the organization in its environment. Objectives are viewed as the essential link between a company and those parts of the environment which are vital for its survival and growth. Decisions rather than activities have most effect on the achievement of objectives. Therefore, the organization structure should provide, above all, communication channels which will facilitate decision-making.

Chapter 3

Writers on Organization: Pre-1939

Frederick Winslow Taylor

F. W. Taylor (1856–1917) joined the Midvale Steel Works in Phila-
delphia as a labourer. He was soon promoted to foreman and then to
Chief Engineer. Later he moved to the Bethlehem Steel Works and later
still he retired from direct management and operated as a consultant.

While at the Midvale plant he applied his engineering training to
the search for more efficient tools for production, and from there he
moved to the wider study of methods of work. His views are recorded
in three main papers, 'Shop Management', written in 1903, 'The
Principles of Scientific Management', written in 1909, and 'Testimony
before the Special House Committee', written in 1912. These three
documents have subsequently been published in one volume, called
Scientific Management.

It is clear to Taylor that the main objective of management 'should
be to secure the maximum prosperity for the employer, coupled with
the maximum prosperity of each employee'. Employer and employee,
therefore, have a basic common interest. But this is not reflected in
practice; we see inefficiency and labour troubles all around. Why?
Taylor gave three causes: the employee's fear of unemployment through
increased productivity, management systems which were to blame for
this fear, and inefficient work methods.

A more scientific approach to management was Taylor's answer to
these problems, and the approach was founded on four basic principles:
first, that a true science of work should be developed. Observation and
measurement should be used to discover what constitutes a fair day's
work. Secondly, men should be scientifically selected and trained to the
work for which they are best suited. Thirdly, the science of work and
the scientific selection and training of men need to be integrated, so that

30

the employee has the opportunity of earning a high rate of pay, while the employer obtains a low cost of production. And finally, there must be constant and willing co-operation between employer and employees to achieve the benefits of scientific management.

The scientific observation and measurement of work led Taylor to believe that greatest efficiency could be achieved by dividing work into its component parts and training men to a very high performance level on individual parts. Maximum specialization was the key. The idea was carried over also into the work of management. Taylor realized that while improving efficiency at the lower levels by specialization, he had greatly expanded the duties of the first-line supervisor. A labourer no longer selected his own tools, set his own pace, used his own method; he did the specialized task at which he could be most efficient. The extraneous, but related, duties became part of the job of first-line supervision. As a solution, Taylor advocated that the principle of specialization was no less appropriate at higher levels than it was at the lowest level. The result was the system called by Taylor 'functional management'. Under this system, each supervisor had a specialist function such as progress control, personnel or maintenance. Taylor proposed that there should be eight supervisors in all, each giving orders directly to the labourers, and each labourer, therefore, having eight bosses.

This idea is Taylor's best known contribution to organization theory; it is also the most harshly criticized. Yet it is a workable system, and even successful companies can have a 'functional' structure.[1]

Taylor's fourth underlying principle of scientific management states that there should be co-operation between employer and employees. It is clear, however, that he felt that management must hold the reins. Co-operation must be enforced where it is not willingly given. Taylor himself says that faster work can only be ensured through 'enforced standardization of methods, enforced adaptation of the best implements and working conditions and enforced co-operation'. And 'management alone' is responsible for this enforcement.

Taylor is probably best known as the founder of work study, and this is certainly his greatest contribution to the theory and practice of

[1] This was one of the findings of the South East Essex Technical College Research Team, reported in Joan Woodward's *Industrial Organization: Theory and Practice*, Oxford Univerity Press, 1965.

management. Out of his search for greater efficiency, however, came ideas with much wider implications. No student of organization can ignore the effects of specialization and 'functional' management on the development of organizations.

Henri Fayol

H. Fayol (1841–1925), like Taylor, was both an engineer by training and an active manager. He worked for the French mining company, Commentry-Fourchamboult-Decazeville, at first as an engineer, then in general management, finally as Managing Director.

Fayol wrote several papers on technical and administrative subjects, but is best known for the single volume *Administration Industrielle et Générale.*

All activities in industrial concerns, Fayol thought, could be divided into six classes. Technical activities dealt with the processes of production, manufacture and adaptation of materials into goods. Commercial activities dealt with the buying, selling and exchange of materials and goods. Financial activities consisted of the search for and best use of capital. Security activities were concerned with the protection of property and personnel. Accounting activities included stocktaking, costing and statistical analysis. Finally, managerial activities consisted of planning, organizing, commanding, co-ordinating and controlling.

This definition of managerial activities is often thought to be Fayol's greatest contribution to administrative theory. It was certainly a unique formulation. He explains the five activities, devoting a chapter of his book to each. To forecast or plan, he says, is to examine the future and evolve a plan of action to meet it. By organization he meant 'building the structure, material and human, of the undertaking'. To command he defined as 'to maintain activity among the personnel'; to co-ordinate is 'to bind together, unifying and harmonizing all activity and effort'; and control he conceived as 'seeing that everything occurs in conformity with established rule and expressed command'.

In any job involving managerial activities Fayol proposed that these five elements would be present to some extent. The higher the level in the organization, the more evident they would be.

It is obvious from *Administration Industrielle et Générale* that Fayol was both very impressed and very unhappy with the state of administrative education. There was, he thought, an over-concentration on the technical aspects of industrial training; engineers needed training in management as well as in their own specialist fields. He attributed the cause to the lack of administrative theory: 'without theory no teaching is possible'. In writing his book he hopes that 'a theory will emanate from it', and he takes the first steps himself by listing and discussing fourteen principles. He emphasizes, however, that these principles must be flexible; 'there is nothing rigid or absolute in administrative affairs; it is all a question of proportion'. The final aim of administrative study will be 'a collection of principles, rules, methods, procedures, tried and checked by general experience'.

Among the fourteen principles, which he expounds in one chapter, are several of direct relevance to the study of organization. These centre around his views on the idea of unity of direction and command, the need for staff specialists, the equation of authority with responsibility, the virtues of informal relationships and the nature of an organization.

Fayol maintains that a 'body with two heads is, in the social as in the animal sphere, a monster that has difficulty in surviving'. He strongly advocates therefore that 'an employee should receive orders from one superior only', and that always there should exist only 'one head and one plan for a group of activities having the same objective'. Fayol recognizes that these principles are often violated in practice and the reasons advanced for dual control are often superficially convincing. But all these companies, in which dual control has 'wormed its way in', have seen the need to eliminate it or have withered away.

Although he criticizes Taylor's solution to the problem of the overload on managers, Fayol agrees that the problem exists. The solution, however, must never be allowed to conflict with the unity of command principle. Fayol's own solution was the need to 'fall back on the staff wherein lies a reserve of physical and mental strength, competence and time on which the manager can draw at will'. He felt that to relieve the overloaded manager the staff should serve as 'an extension of the manager's personality'. To enable them to function effectively they should be free from 'all responsibility for running the business'.

The freedom of staff specialists from all such responsibility would entitle them to no authority in the operating functions, since Fayol felt most strongly that authority should be matched with responsibility. He defined authority as 'the right to give orders and the power to exact

33

obedience'. It was essential, he thought, to be certain about the amount of responsibility of all those who had authority, since people naturally seek more authority and avoid responsibility. If this is allowed, chaos results. Yet he realized the difficulties, since 'the measurement of this responsibility and its equivalent in material terms elude all calculation'.

Impressed though he was with the need for a formal structure, with a definite chain of command and man-to-man responsibility, Fayol recognized the value of certain informal relationships. He realized that to insist that communications between two subordinates in different departments go through departmental heads would be slow and wasteful of managerial effort. There was no reason why the subordinates should not have direct contact, as long as their immediate superiors authorized the relationship and were kept informed. This provision would accelerate communication without violating the line of authority. It would also, Fayol implies, make different departments more aware of their essential interaction.

Fayol saw danger in viewing an organization as an 'administrative machine'. He insisted that every executive in a company 'must be a generator of ideas and power'. The machine concept implies that the administrative 'gearing . . . is incapable of transmitting movement without losing power'. Fayol himself compares the organization structure to a 'body corporate'. Management is the nervous system of the animal, and the growth of the animal is determined both by the strength of its nervous system and the activities of other animals.

To see the state of the animal at any time Fayol recommends the use of organization charts, 'a precious managerial instrument'. By this means the company ensures that every employee has a place and sees that he is in his appointed place. It can also show strengths and weaknesses, and the effects of changes.

Fayol, unlike Taylor, looked down on the organization from a management viewpoint almost from the beginning of his career. He was never as deeply involved as Taylor in the production process. The result is a broader scope and a less definitive treatment. Taylor's principles were the result of 'scientific observation and measurement', Fayol's of personal experience over many years of management practice.

Fayol's greatest contribution was the unique definition of the nature of management. But this definition is of less concern in the present study than his principles concerning unity of command, staff specialists,

34

informal relationships and the nature of organizations. These themes are taken up again and again in the literature of organization.

Max Weber

M. Weber (1864–1920) studied law and, after qualifying, joined the teaching staff at Berlin University. Unlike both Taylor and Fayol, therefore, he had an academic background, and in fact he remained an academic for the rest of his life.

His main studies concerned the sociology of organization and religion, and these two were combined in his best known work in translation, *The Protestant Ethic and the Spirit of Capitalism*. He wrote very many other works, the most important of which, for our purposes, are *The Theory of Social and Economic Organization*, a book which Weber obviously intended as his *magnum opus* but which was unfinished at his death, and a collection of his works translated and edited by H. H. Gerth and C. Wright Mills, entitled *From Max Weber: Essays in Sociology*.

The difference between Weber on the one hand, and Taylor and Fayol on the other, is basically a difference of approach. Weber, unlike his two contemporaries, had not the urgency of practical problems of organization compelling him to seek solutions. As a result, his writings tend not to be prescriptive, merely descriptive. His first thought is not to say what the basis of organization should be, but merely to analyse what it is.

Weber felt that the fundamental questions we have to answer about organizations concern the recognition and use of authority. What is authority and what is it about authority that makes subordinates accept the exercise of power by superiors? Weber answered these questions by the separation and analysis of three 'ideal' types of authority structure, which he called 'charismatic', 'traditional' and 'rational-legal' or 'bureaucratic'.

The word 'charisma' appears in the writings of the early Christians. Literally it means 'gift of grace'. A charismatic leader, therefore, is one who leads by virtue of some exceptional innate quality. The concept has overtones of the superhuman and supernatural; charismatic leaders would include prophets, warrior-chiefs and heads of religious sects. The power that the leader holds is purely the result of his personal charisma; and he can remain in power as long as his charisma is accepted by and satisfies his followers.

An organization built on the personal charisma of one man has a natural instability. Rarely does a successor have a charisma that will stand the comparison with the man he replaces. More often the authority structure will become one based on heredity or procedures and rules. It will become a 'traditional' or 'rational-legal' organization.

When a charismatic leader dies and his son replaces him, authority tends to become part of the leader's role, not part of his personality. The authority of the leadership role is accepted because of precedent. It comes to depend on 'an established belief in the sanctity of immemorial traditions and the legitimacy of the status of those exercising authority under them'. The strongest justification for an act is that 'things have always been done that way'.

The word 'bureaucracy' has for us many connotations which Weber never envisaged. He felt that the bureaucratic organization was by its very nature the most efficient form of organization. 'Rational-legal' was his first name for it; it was rational in that specific objectives were laid down and the organization designed to achieve these objectives; and it was legal because authority stemmed from a clearly defined set of rules, procedures and roles. Authority is clearly the possession of the job, not of the man. The systems established are those most likely to achieve the organization's goals, not those in which one man is interested, nor those which 'have always existed'.

In a pure bureaucracy, according to Weber, work is divided into a set of clearly defined spheres of responsibility. Each sphere is the sole occupation of one man, and, although he holds the authority to perform the office, he does so by virtue of his technical ability to perform the necessary tasks. His appointment is a matter of contract freely entered into.

There is a clear separation between subordinate and superior levels. The manifestations of this are that higher offices supervise lower ones; there are different degrees of social esteem recognized for each level; there are different, fixed salaries paid at each level; seniority and ability determine inter-level promotion; and there is provision for appeals to higher levels.

Finally, personal and official matters are clearly divorced. Personal considerations of gratitude and favour do not enter into business decisions. Each office carries an obligation to act in accordance with clearly defined objectives and procedures.

It is this tendency to eliminate the personal which makes Weber despair of bureaucracy, despite its alleged efficiency. In a debate he once said, 'It is horrible to think that the world could one day be filled with nothing but those little cogs, little men clinging to little jobs and striving towards bigger ones. . . . '[1] There were to be many other voices raised in agreement.

Weber's work ranged over a very wide field. On the subject of organization, he is important for having attempted the first classification of organizations, and for his penetrating study of bureaucracy.

Mary Parker Follett

M. P. Follett (1868–1933) studied political science and economics at Harvard and Cambridge. She was very active in social work especially among young people, and helped to develop educational and recreational centres and set up vocational guidance committees. Her work in youth employment and vocational guidance brought her into close contact with industry and commerce, where she found that managers were facing and, on the whole, coping better with the same problems as public administrators.

Follett's writings, like Weber's, covered a wide field. In *The New State* she deals with government and community work. The psychology of conflicting groups is the subject of *Creative Experience*. She presented her ideas on administration and organization in a series of papers and lectures which have been collected and edited by Metcalf and Urwick in the book *Dynamic Administration, the Collected Papers of Mary Parker Follett*.

It is difficult to summarize Follett's views and to integrate them into a general theory of organization. In any case, the attempt to do so would have horrified Follett herself, who felt most strongly that social interaction is a constantly changing and evolving phenomenon. There are, however, a number of ideas central to her philosophy of organization. We shall consider some of these: the question of power and authority, 'cumulative responsibility', the 'law of the situation', 'constructive conflict' and 'four principles of co-ordination'.

[1] Quoted in *Max Weber, An Intellectual Portrait* by R. Bendix.

COMPANY ORGANIZATION THEORY AND PRACTICE

Follett criticizes writers who talk about power as if it were 'a pre-existing thing which can be handed out to someone, or wrenched from someone . . .'. Power, she says, is 'simply the ability to make things happen, to be a causal agent, to initiate change'. Such ability is a personal possession of the manager; he cannot share, separate, confer or transfer it. He can merely give his subordinates 'an opportunity for developing their power'. The aim of every man should be 'more power for the best furtherance of that activity . . . to which we are giving our life'. But, although power is a personal possession, it is strongest when it is 'power with' others, not 'power over' others; it must be co-operative and collective power.

Authority is power vested in individuals, not, however, in individuals as persons, but in individuals as performers of functions. Authority, therefore, can be conferred, just as the duty of performing the function is conferred. 'Authority', says Follett, 'belongs to the job and stays with the job.' No manager, therefore, should have 'more authority than goes with his function', and because of this Follett cannot see how a man can delegate authority unless he delegates at least part of his function.

Since authority 'belongs to the job', responsibility too must be an attribute of the job. People should not be responsible to someone, but rather responsible *for* something. If, however, responsibility is as diffuse as the functions to which it is attached, how can activities in an organization be harmonized? Follett's answer is the concept of collective and cumulative responsibility. It is collective in that several people are responsible for the achievement of the same objectives. It is cumulative in that it should start at the lowest levels and build up into a company-wide pattern. The emphasis is greater on horizontal relationships than on vertical relationships, the chain of command. 'Strand should weave with strand, and then we shall not have the clumsy task of trying to patch together finished webs.' We may say that it is better for the salesman to work with the line supervisor who manufactures for his part of the market, than it is for the Sales and Production Directors to force co-operation between their departments from the top. Every member of the organization, therefore, shares in the task of co-ordination as he shares in the responsibility for results.

Follett felt, however, that the difficulty envisaged as a result of collective responsibility should never arise. If functions are clearly

38

defined, we have a basis for deciding who is responsible for failure. But the determination of responsibility for failure is not a means to apportion blame, it simply assists us to do better in the future.

How people in organizations should be controlled was a general question of great interest to Follett. Others felt that control had to be direct and personal to be effective. It was typical of Follett that she criticized the concept of one man controlling another. Both, she said, were subject to an impersonal law – the 'law of the situation'. Two people should examine the problem and take action as the conditions demand. 'The head of the sales department does not give orders to the head of the production department, or vice versa. Each studies the market and the final decision is made as the market demands.'

Her deep interest in the then new tool of psychology obviously led Follett to this solution. People, she realized, cannot be 'bossed' into doing things. 'The more you are "bossed", the more your activity of thought will take place within the bossing pattern and your part in that pattern seems usually to be opposition to the bossing.' It is no surprise therefore that she thought that the 'law of the situation' should determine action not simply between equals, but between superior and subordinate. Orders 'should be the composite decision of those who give and those who receive them'.

Once again from her interest in psychology, Follett was aware that conflict is bound to arise in groups, and, since her philosophy of organization envisages group authority and responsibility, the question of conflict figures prominently in her writings.

In one of her essays, 'Constructive Conflict', she proposes three ways in which we can handle the problem of conflicting views within a group. First, one view can dominate; this entails a waste of time and effort by the supporters of other views. Second, there can be a compromise; no side gains a victory and all views may lose their sharpness and bite. Third, the views can be integrated; all sides can be represented and the whole may be better than the sum of its parts.

This is Follett's answer to the problem of making conflict a constructive element in group interaction. It is essentially dependent on people having the 'power-with' rather than the 'power-over' attitude.

Follett's views on co-ordination are expressed very clearly when she talks of 'collective planning'. The instrument of collective planning is co-ordination which is the 'reciprocal relating of all the factors in a situation'. We have met this idea before, an idea which is far more evocative of co-operation than the usual 'pressure from above'. There are three additional principles for collective planning laid down by Follett. First, there should be direct contact between the people whose activities need to be co-ordinated. Second, co-ordination must start in the very early stages before policies have been completely formed. This ties in very closely with Follett's idea that every level in the organization has a policy-making role. And finally, co-ordination should be a continuing process, like the social interaction which is its backcloth.

Follett's thinking was fundamentally different from the three writers we have previously discussed. She seems to have taken as her first concern the question – what is the most efficient use of people? She used the new tool of psychology; and the answers she produced have given her a deserved reputation as pioneer of the Human Relations approach.

Elton Mayo

E. Mayo (1880–1949) trained as a medical student but soon abandoned this to follow his interests in psychology and philosophy. An Australian by birth, he went to the United States and joined the staff of Harvard University, eventually becoming Professor of Industrial Research at Harvard Graduate School of Business Studies.

His interest, like Follett's, was primarily in the people in organizations. His two most widely read books reflect this interest: *The Human Problems of an Industrial Civilization* and *The Social Problems of an Industrial Civilization*.

Mayo is best known for his work on the project which is commonly referred to as the Hawthorne Studies. In 1927 an extensive investigation was started at the Hawthorne plant, near Chicago, of the Western Electric Company. The initial brief was to examine the effects of fatigue on workers, but this was greatly extended, and it was not until five years later that the project was finished. During this time Fritz Roethlisberger acted as research assistant to Mayo; and the book, *Management and the Worker*, written by Roethlisberger and W. J. Dickson of Western Electric, is another essential source for details about the Hawthorne Studies.

The first phase of the Hawthorne Studies was an experiment involving five girls engaged on electrical assembly testing. The researchers separ-
40

ated the girls from the rest of the labour force; they were placed in a special room which came to be known as the Relay Assembly Test Room. A supervisor was installed with them to keep records and maintain a friendly atmosphere.

Over a period of a year and a half various improvements were introduced in the working environment and conditions. Rest periods were extended; the working week was reduced from 48 hours to below 42. Each change brought an increase in hourly output; so much so that it was not until the working week was reduced below 42 hours that the weekly output showed a drop.

These results probably did not surprise the researchers, since even if there was no evidence to support it there was a feeling that improved working conditions would increase output. As the next step, however, the improvements were systematically removed from the Relay Assembly Test Room. Rest periods were withdrawn and the girls reverted to working a 48-hour week. Hourly output fell a little but was still much higher than it had been at the beginning of the experiment, with the result that with the reintroduction of the 48-hour week output climbed above all previous levels.

Finally, the improvements were reintroduced. Output soared, so that even working 42 hours per week the girls produced more than they had ever done before.

These effects baffled the researchers. They could not explain what was the constant element which stimulated the girls to increase output even when seemingly adverse changes were made in the working environment and conditions. Various avenues were explored. Could it be explained (as Taylor might have tried to explain it) by financial incentives? In the Relay Assembly Test Room the girls' bonus was based on the work of their group of five, not as previously on the output of about one hundred others. Could the more personal incentive have had these effects? To test this a further experimental group was set up, identical to the first in every respect except for the incentive scheme. The girls in this second group were paid bonuses on an even more personal, in fact, an individual basis. But the results of this second group were disappointing and convinced the research team that neither incentives nor 'all the itemized changes experimentally imposed . . . could . . . be used to explain the major change – the continually increasing production'.

In an attempt to get background information which might explain the results received from the Relay Assembly Test Room, Mayo and his team conducted an interview programme throughout the factory. It was hoped that this might reveal significant facts about the working conditions. The researchers soon realized, however, that the interviews tended to show more of the interviewee's attitudes to his work, his supervisor and his company, than it did facts about these things. According to Roethlisberger and Dickson, 'the latent content of a statement, that is, the attitude of the complainant, was just as important to understand as its manifest content'.

As an attempt to discover facts, therefore, the survey was often a failure. But a number of benefits did come as a result; morale seemed to be improved since the employees 'appreciated being recognized as individuals who had valuable comments to make'; the attitudes of supervisors were improved since each began to feel that 'his methods were being made the subject of research and . . . his subordinates were being invited to express their opinions about him'; and finally the researchers, for their part, learnt the importance of workers' attitudes and feelings. To quote Roethlisberger, they discovered that the social structure was 'an intricate web of human relations bound together by a system of sentiments'.

The third and last stage in the Hawthorne Studies consisted of an investigation into the work practices of a non-experimental group, consisting of fourteen men and four supervisors. These employees worked in the Bank Wiring Observation Room; the operatives were under constant supervision and their output was carefully recorded. It was soon clear that they were restricting their output, despite an individually-based incentive scheme. A closer examination of work practice and attitudes revealed that there was a definite code of conduct operating among these employees. Output was set at a level which was, to the operatives, a medium between 'rate-busting' (producing too much) and 'chiselling' (producing too little).

'Squealing' to supervisors was not permitted, and a man who 'kept to himself' was suspected. Those who were strongest in conforming to these norms were recognized by the group as their leaders. It was clear that the attachment to this 'informal' organization was stronger than both the individual's desire for greater earnings and the company's formal requirements.

Returning to the research in the Relay Assembly Test Room, we can now attempt to explain the continually increasing output of the female operatives. First, the girls formed a closely knit group; they co-operated happily with the researchers and each other. Second, they had group norms of willingness and co-operation. These were engendered by the joint consultation which took place before changes were introduced and by the relaxed nature of supervision. The operatives were allowed to feel that they were governing their own fate to a large extent. Third and last, the girls became the object of great attention, inside and outside the plant. This had due effect on the pride they took in their work.

The Hawthorne Studies have had a shattering impact on management thinking. The 'rabble hypothesis', that everyone pursues his own individual self-interest, had to be tempered in the light of Mayo's 'discovery' of the 'informal' organization of groups. The idea that man was an adjunct to a machine had to give ground to the proven importance of workers' feelings and attitudes. And the drive for efficiency had henceforth to be backed up by an understanding of the human factor at work.

Chapter 4

Writers on Organization: Post-1939

Lyndall F. Urwick

In a long and varied career, L. F. Urwick gained vast experience both of military and civil organization. He has been a director of the International Management Institute at Geneva and he was for some time head of a management consultancy company.

His recorded talks and published works on management subjects are too numerous to list in full. On organization his most important publications are: *Papers on the Science of Administration* (edited jointly by Urwick and Luther Gulick who each submitted two of the papers), *The Elements of Administration, The Making of Scientific Management* (in three volumes, written by Urwick and E. F. L. Brech) and *A Short Survey of Industrial Management*.

It would not be too harsh to say that there is little that is new in the writings of Urwick. He relies heavily on earlier writers, especially Fayol, Taylor and Follett, both for the concepts they evolved and the mistakes they made. He borrows from and criticizes their work in his attempt to develop broad principles of administration, a body of knowledge and a set of rules.

The influence of Taylor and Fayol is clear in Urwick's basic approach to organization. Urwick was certain of one thing: rationality should take precedence over personality. 'I am convinced', he says, 'that a logical scheme of organization, a structure based on principles, which take priority over personalities, is in the long run far better both for the morale of an undertaking as a whole and for the happiness of individuals, than the attempt to build one's organization around persons.' Accordingly he defines organizing as 'determining what activities are necessary to any purpose . . . and arranging them in groups which may be assigned to individuals'. This should be done in a spirit of

44

detachment, and only when the rational, efficient, optimum structure has been designed, should we consider personalities; only then should we try to fit people to, or find people for, the structure.

What are the principles, then, on which the structure is to be based? First, specialization is a key concept for Urwick, just as it was for Taylor; 'let the cobbler stick to his last' had meaning for both of them, but not precisely the same meaning. Urwick, in at least one passage, explains a reservation he has about specialization. He says that because Henry Ford had been successful with conveyor belt assembly, people were apt to exaggerate the advantages of very minute subdivision of processes. He complains that the job can be reduced to a level where it requires no skill or intelligence, and then the danger is of 'error begotten of boredom'. Urwick was, therefore, conscious of the problems created by over-specialization. Even so he still supports the principle, tending to modify it from minute subdivision to specialization of function. This leads to the concept that there should be three kinds of formal relations in organization: line relations (closely related to the chain of command), functional relations (where departments supply a specialized service such as Personnel), and staff relations.

To Urwick the solution of the problem of relationships between line and staff was to define two distinct types of staff personnel. On the one hand, there are staff specialists: finance, legal, personnel experts. Their main activities consist of planning, reading, thinking and advising. They have no authority in the accepted sense; they get results by personal persuasion. On the other hand, we have the general staff. Their major task is to lighten the burden of the chief executive by assisting in the details of command, control and co-ordination. They can co-ordinate the work of specialists but they are not themselves experts in any speciality.

Urwick realizes that the difficulty of staff taking line authority still exists even with his two types of staff. In military organizations, he says, it is clear that the general staff's actions are 'in virtue of their appointment ... and involve no assertion of unjustified authority'. There is no indication, however, of the way in which the concept of staff with line authority can be made acceptable in the non-military organization.

Perhaps the answer is to be found in the Principle of Definition. In line with his basic approach of rationality, Urwick proposes that

45

authority must be clearly defined, preferably in writing. Everyone should know his responsibilities and the relationship of himself to others and others to himself.

Fayol stated that authority should be matched by responsibility. Urwick takes up the point when he says that executives must delegate 'the necessary authority to discharge the responsibility'. Furthermore, men in responsible positions must also be 'personally accountable for all actions taken by their subordinates'. And, despite Fayol's doubt about the measurability of authority and responsibility, Urwick summarizes by saying that 'authority and responsibility should be coterminous and co-equal'.

Urwick also adopted Fayol's principles of the Unity of Command and the Span of Control. In support of the former, he enthusiastically quotes a United States Government report on organization and administration: 'The conspicuously well-managed administrative units in the Government are almost without exception headed by single administrators.' Committees have a place, but it is not their function to administrate.

The argument for a restricted Span of Control hangs on the number of interrelationships in the team consisting of the supervisor and his subordinates. This idea is advanced by V. A. Graicunas, a French mathematician, who wrote the paper 'Relationship in Organization', which is included in *Papers on the Science of Administration*. Urwick supported the view of Graicunas that relationships which require the attention of the supervisor can be seen to increase in a geometrical progression with the increase in numbers of subordinates. For example, if there are six subordinates, the number of interrelationships among his subordinates which require the supervisor's attention can be as many as 222. Urwick maintains, therefore, that at the middle and higher levels in the organization a supervisor should not have more than five or at most six subordinates whose work interlocks. The lower levels, however, provide an exception: here the number 'may be eight or twelve', since at this level it is the responsibility for the performance of specific tasks which is delegated, not the responsibility for supervising the work of others.

On the question of delegation, Urwick felt strongly that the man who lacked the courage to delegate was heading for failure. In larger organizations, he maintained, it will even be necessary to delegate the

46

right to delegate. And, once a task has been passed down the chain of command, the executive ultimately responsible should 'manage by exception', only involving himself when there are significant deviations from the plan.

Despite his emphasis on a rational, prescribed procedure for organizational relations, Urwick, like Fayol, realized the advantages of the less formal relationships in an organization. 'Lateral' relationships between people in different departments are permitted to develop within the formal framework. As Urwick himself said, 'It is both right and proper that every organization should have its formal scalar chain, just as every well-built house has its drainage system. But it is unnecessary to use the formal channels exclusively or primarily as the sole means of communication as it is unnecessary to pass one's time in the drains.'

Urwick is without doubt one of the most prolific writers and propagandists of views on administration. The fact that there is little real innovation in his ideas on organization should not detract from his well-deserved reputation as an administrative pioneer. He surveyed a very wide field and greatly clarified and made explicit many of the thoughts of his predecessors and contemporaries. These are his contributions to our subject.

E. F. L. Brech

E. F. L. Brech has been a consultant colleague of Urwick and a co-author with him of several books. Like his senior partner, he has mainly elaborated or clarified the views of earlier writers.

In the preface to his most important book, *Organization: The Framework of Management*, he sets out his reasons for writing. He feels that the book will fulfil a need for a 'single explanation of the nature of organization structure'. Previous publications on the whole have concentrated on specific cases, or, where they have generalized, have been 'complex and thus difficult as a source from which the practising Manager can draw immediate lessons'. Often one leaves conferences and study groups with the impression of having been present at a 'shadow-boxing' session. It is Brech's intention, therefore, to try to formalize a completely practical approach based on tried, general principles. He sees the necessity for this not only to fill the gap in the present literature, but as a result of the growing feeling that organization

47

is a 'major factor in determining efficient operation'. And furthermore, increasing interest in 'executive development' will force companies to make a clear 'delineation of specific areas of responsibility to which the growing executive can be accredited, and within which his skills can be developed and nurtured'.

In many respects, Brech shows himself to be more aware than Urwick of the human relations aspects of organization; when he talks of the relationships between superior and subordinate, the word 'command' has given way to the word 'motivate'; more attention is given to the personal satisfactions of employees. In the twenty years between 1940 and 1960, there was much activity on the human relations front, and much criticism of the 'formal principles' of earlier writers as a result. Brech's deepest sympathies obviously lie with the 'formal' school, and equally obviously he felt the need to answer the criticisms and where necessary alter principles in the light of current thought.

For example, on the Span of Control principle he is less definitive than his predecessors. 'The span of responsibility or supervision of a superior should be limited to a reasonable number of executive or supervisory subordinates if their activities are interrelated.' The prescribed number is not four, five or six, but depends on the ability of the manager and the demands of his supervisory and other tasks. And it is clearly implied that the Span of Control only needs to be limited where the supervisor is responsible for the work of other supervisors, not at the lowest level in the organization.

Brech agreed with Urwick that there should be only one man at the top. 'An organization should provide . . . a single chief executive responsible to the policy-forming body for the effective conduct of all operations of the enterprise.' He should strike a balance between the units and co-ordinate their activities. He must also set the tone of the enterprise.

Brech also gives clear definitions of the various functions and relationships of elements in the organization. There are first 'the relations of the senior to his subordinates, and vice versa'. Such relations are 'those of instruction and compliance, in the customary sense in which a higher authority may give valid orders to those within its jurisdiction', and are often referred to as 'line' or 'direct' relations.

Secondly, we have the 'relations of the specialist positions or personnel to the "line" managers and subordinates who are served or assisted by the specialist activities'. The specialists have a responsibility for a service, but have no authority over those who use this service. A specialist manager may, however, have a line authority over members of his own specialist department. He also has a line relationship with his own superior. His relations with other personnel, however, are of an 'indirect' nature; he is a specialist 'adviser', but, since his advice is sanctioned by higher management, all those whom it concerns must accept it. The relations of these managers to other personnel are often called 'functional'.

Thirdly, there are 'staff relations'. Here Brech adopts Urwick's idea of the 'general staff', a concept which he feels should be encouraged. A 'staff officer' is appointed as a personal assistant to a higher manager. But 'the personal assistant or "general staff officer" has no authority or responsibility in his own right at all'. He is 'little more than an extension of the personality he serves'. His relations with other personnel cannot be described since, as himself, he has none.

Finally, there are 'lateral relations'. These are the relations implying co-operation between executives on the same organizational level in different units of the organization. Each executive 'can fulfil his own role effectively only if he maintains contact and collaboration with colleagues whose responsibilities are essentially related to his own'. Such relations may be laid down formally, but their effectiveness depends on the attitudes of the executives; they are, therefore, more dependent on 'management' than organization.

In a sense 'lateral relations' are 'informal relations', which 'are the reflection of the "attitude of responsible mutual co-operation" which every member of an organization should be expected to display as an essential feature in management skill'. Informal relations, however, can be negative; they can be typified by conflict and opposition. Brech sees a difference, however, between 'informal relations', as defined above, and the 'informal organization' that was revealed in the Hawthorne Studies. Informal relations refer only 'to members of an organization structure and to their mutual association in regard to activities arising out of the formal pattern of respective responsibilities'. The informal organization Brech sees as 'a purely personal social affinity', having 'no regard to the structure in which it is set, nor any concern with the responsibilities'.

Finally, we will consider Brech's views on authority and responsibility.

49

In his discussion of these related concepts he criticizes Urwick for the need to formulate the principle that 'responsibility and authority be coterminous and co-equal.' 'It is questionable', he says, 'whether there is need to identify a "principle" in this direction.' Brech's own feeling is that delegation cannot be meaningful unless an executive has 'authority to carry out the responsibilities allocated'; 'if the responsibilities are, in fact, allocated, he automatically gets the authority necessary to carry them out'. If an executive were able to ask his subordinates to be accountable for certain duties without giving them authority, he would not be delegating responsibility, but merely giving them 'instructions to perform detailed duties on the basis of his own decisions'.

The difficulty has arisen, says Brech, through the lack of written definitions of responsibilities. To give a man 'responsibility as a Works Manager' is so vague an idea that discrepancies between the man's and his superior's conception of what the responsibility involves are bound to occur. 'Once, however, a responsibility is defined . . . the grant of appropriate authority commensurate therewith is implicit in the definition of responsibility, i.e. the granting of authority is automatic.'

The key to effective organization, therefore, is clear definition of responsibilities Brech sums up his philosophy on this question in the following words: 'It is the contention of the present author that the responsibilities of management forming an organization structure should always be written down in properly constituted standards or "schedules". This, it is maintained, is the only practical means of delegation, the only effective way of making known the patterns of responsibilities and relationships, both to the holders of the positions concerned and to all others who together form the management team.'

Brech, like his colleague Urwick, surveyed the whole field of management. Brech himself selected from and adopted a number of Urwick's principles, just as Urwick had done to the work of his predecessors. The result is that we have in Brech's writings one of the most sophisticated and comprehensive formulations of the 'Classical approach' to organization.

Peter F. Drucker
Drucker's background in Austria and Germany included law and journalism. With the growth of Nazism he moved to London, then to

New York, and operated as a business consultant. One of his best known works is the book *Concept of the Corporation* published in 1946, dealing with the organization and management of General Motors. He has written many other books on management subjects, including *Practice of Management* which has been, and still is, something of a best seller.

General Motors is typical of the type of company that Drucker finds most interesting. He is not concerned by the fact that such giants are comparatively few in number, since for him they seem to 'embody the spirit' of modern industry. Consequently, his ideas on organization tend to be largely based upon the practices of large corporations.

As with Brech, it is essentially in the practical field that Drucker wishes to stimulate advances. In the opening paragraphs of Part III of *Practice of Management*, he draws a parallel between the organization theorist who talks about how the structure should be built and a civil engineer who 'discusses the relative advantages and limitations of cantilever and suspension bridges'. But the manager wants to know what kind of structure he needs, and the civil authorities want to know 'whether they should build a highway and from where to where'. Both approaches are relevant, but 'only confusion can result if the question what kind of a road should be built is answered with a discussion of the structural stresses and strains of various types of bridge'. It is Drucker's intention, therefore, to try to answer both questions: what kind of structure is needed and how it should be built.

Organization for Drucker is a means to the 'end of business performance and business results'. The first questions, therefore, should be: 'What is our business and what should it be?' Then the organization must be designed to attain the objectives of the business, and Drucker recommends three ways of discovering what kind of structure will help attain the objectives: activities analysis; decisions analysis; relations analysis.

Drucker criticizes earlier writers for neglecting the real 'activities analysis'. They labelled functions, such as 'manufacturing', 'engineering' or 'selling', but omitted to define what these consisted of and how large a part they played in attaining the objectives of the business. Drucker gives examples of how in specific businesses certain activities assume an importance which is essential to the success of the business, but which could easily be neglected by a less enlightened management.

51

He concludes by saying that 'they were organized as separate functions because an activities analysis revealed that as part of another function they were not being given the attention their importance warranted'. An activities analysis should, therefore, 'bring out what work has to be performed, what kinds of work belong together, and what emphasis each activity is to be given in the organization structure'.

The second set of questions to be answered in designing an organization structure concerns the decisions to be made. Drucker sees no great difficulty in anticipating the kinds of decisions that will arise. In one company he found that over 90 per cent of the decisions that managers had to take over a period of five years were 'typical' decisions and 'fell within a small number of categories'.

The nature of business decisions is determined by four characteristics: 'the degree of futurity in the decision' – for how long will it commit the company?; 'the impact a decision has on other functions'; 'the number of qualitative factors that enter into it' – how much does it depend on ethical values, politics, etc.?; and 'whether they are periodically recurrent or rare'. Analysing decisions in this way, we can determine the level at which they should be taken. For example, a decision to build a new plant commits the company heavily, affects many departments, may involve the company in dealings with local authorities and certainly does not occur every day. Such a decision should be made at a high level.

'The final step in the analysis of structure is an analysis of relations.' Drucker criticizes traditional thinking for defining a manager's relations only in a downward direction. We should first consider his contribution 'to the larger unit of which he is a part'. We must also analyse the 'sideways relations', since 'the contribution which a manager makes to the managers of other activities is always an important part of his job and may be the most important one'. The object of analysing relations is not only to help define the structure but also to give guidance in manning the structure.

As he moves from questions about the kind of structure to the problem of building the structure Drucker outlines what he calls three 'structural requirements of the enterprise'. First, 'it must be organized for business performance' – the criterion is the attainment of the right objectives. Second, it should 'contain the least possible number of management levels' – for simplicity, for direction, for effectiveness and for the development of personnel. Third, it must make possible the training and testing of tomorrow's top managers – giving responsibility to the manager while he is still young and in positions where failure would not endanger the business. In line with these requirements, he discusses two structural principles: 'federal decentralization' and 'functional decentralization'. Of these, the former is preferable and should be applied wherever possible. It involves the organization of activities into autonomous product businesses, each with its own market and product and with its own profit and loss responsibility. Where federal decentralization is not possible a business must use 'functional decentralization, which sets up integrated units with maximum responsibility for a major and distinct stage in the business process'. Drucker gives a very detailed account of the pros and cons of each principle; we will not, however, discuss them further at this stage, since they will form a very large part of our later discussion of decentralization. There is no doubt, however, that decentralization, especially federal decentralization, as Drucker envisages it, provides the greatest opportunities for satisfying his three 'structural requirements': performance can be set and measured, management levels can be few, and there is scope for training the managers of tomorrow.

In this brief survey it has been possible only to give the core of Drucker's thinking on organization. He equals both Urwick and Brech in the scope and volume of his work in this field. However, his writings are often considered more modern and popular than theirs. This may be the consequence of the greater appeal and 'glamour' of the examples which he can quote from his own experience, but it is more likely to be the fact that companies are applying with considerable success the principles which he proposed.

Herbert A. Simon

Simon is an American political and social scientist. He started his career in local government where, at the age of twenty-two, he published his first article, 'Measuring Municipal Activities', written in conjunction with Clarence Ridley. He became interested in general theories of organization and his study in this field led to the publication of several books and articles, including *Administrative Behaviour* (1947: second edition 1960), *Public Administration* (1950: with D. Smithburg and V.

53

Thompson), *Organizations* (1958: with James G. March) and *The New Science of Management Decision* (1960).

Simon was clearly influenced in his early work by his predecessors. He made no attempt to conceal his disgust at the way in which the glib phrases and 'homely proverbs' of writers such as Urwick and Luther Gulick were accepted. He attacked many of the 'principles' of the Classical school. He pointed out that a limited Span of Control was in conflict with the equally (if not more) laudable maxim of 'keeping at a minimum the number of organizational levels through which a matter must pass before it is acted upon'. The principle of Unity of Command if acted out would only reduce efficiency, since, if the 'advice' of specialists had to be passed down the chain of command, this would waste time and managerial effort.

In more recent years, however, Simon has concentrated his attention on a more specialized field. His attempts to measure the efficiency of various methods of local government led him to the study of operational research. Most recently he has been engaged on research into the human processes of decision-making using computers to simulate human thinking.

Management to Simon means decision-making. He postulates three stages in the decision-making process. Stage one he calls the 'intelligence activity' – discovering when and where it is necessary to make a decision. Stage two is the 'design activity' – finding and developing alternative courses of action. And stage three consists of the 'choice activity' – actually making the selection from the alternatives available. Each stage may itself require complete decision-making cycles; for example, it will be necessary to decide when to call off the search for alternatives. Again, when the choice activity is complete a new set of decisions has to be made about implementation, and so on. It is easy to envisage how decision-making can be involved in everything a manager does, and that all three stages must be worked through, consciously or subconsciously.

While talking of the decision-making process, Simon criticizes those who imply that man is completely rational. Traditional theories of economics and statistical decision-making assume that people who make decisions know all possible outcomes, that their powers of calculation are sufficient and that they have a constant set of criteria by which they can evaluate alternatives. Simon suggests that since none of these three assumptions has any validity, a man cannot be said to be solving his problems with optimal solutions, but rather with solutions which are satisfactory or 'good enough'. Man cannot 'maximize', so he 'satisfies'.

Man is not, therefore, a completely rational animal, he has only 'bounded rationality'. But how does this affect organization? Simon's answer is that the environment in which management operates must be designed such that 'the individual will approach as close as practicable to rationality (judged in terms of the organization's goals) in his decisions'. The organization and methods should be such that managers will tend as far as possible to make the best decisions rather than decisions which are 'good enough'.

In this discussion of how decision-making can be improved, Simon distinguishes between two extreme types of decision, programmed and unprogrammed. Any decisions can be placed on a continuum between the fully programmed and the completely unprogrammed. A decision which approximates to the programmed end of the continuum would be one for which there is a prescribed procedure, such as the decision when and how much to reorder when buying materials for an established product with a steady market over a number of years. Or it may be a question of simple routine, requiring no conscious thought, as such.

The greater the precedent and the more widely held the knowledge about the precedent, the more programmed the decision will be. Conversely, if there is no precedent, no experience to go on, the more unprogrammed will be the decision. As an example we may quote the decision to launch a new product in a company which has grown up with only one product. Here there may be subsidiary decisions which are programmed and so contribute to the rationality of the overall decision, but the essence of the decision to launch or not to launch is still very much a question of hunch or intuition.

The intelligence of human beings can compensate partially for the unprogrammed nature of some decisions. Solutions can be found which are a satisfactory approximation to rationality, i.e. to optimal solutions. But it is inefficient to rely on the intelligence of human beings when decisions can be programmed. According to Simon, therefore, an enterprise should programme as many decisions as possible by encouraging habits, knowledge and skills, or by installing clerical procedures and routines, or by building the right organization structure and values.

55

Simon sees and tries to anticipate the criticism of the Human Relations school who would object to maximum standardization and installation of routines. He says: 'A completely unstructured situation, to which one can apply only the most general problem-solving skills, without specific rules or direction, is, if prolonged, painful for most people. Routine is a welcome refuge from the trackless forests of unfamiliar problem spaces.'

With the growing use of the computer, however, Simon sees the possibility of programming what was previously a completely unprogrammed decision, by simulating human thought processes. 'The automated factory of the future will operate on the basis of programmed decisions produced in the automated office beside it.'

Although much of Simon's work concentrates on management, not organization, the implications of his hypotheses and predictions have a direct bearing on the framework within which management operates. Despite his early criticisms of the Classical school, he would agree with them that the criterion of organizational success is efficiency. And efficiency will increase as the 'bounded rationality' of man is replaced by the total rationality of routine using the electronic computer.

Douglas McGregor

McGregor was an American social psychologist who conducted a variety of research projects into the motivation and general behaviour of people in organizations. He was until his recent death Professor of Management at Massachusetts Institute of Technology.

The most widely publicized aspect of McGregor's work is his distinction between two basic theories of human behaviour at work. In his book, *The Human Side of Enterprise*, he describes these two views, which he calls Theory X and Theory Y.

Traditional theories about the way in which administration should work were based on Theory X. Theory X assumes that the average worker is lazy and dislikes work. He is unambitious, avoids responsibility and prefers to be led. He is selfish, having no concern for organizational objectives. He must, therefore, be controlled, coerced and directed, if the organization is to achieve its objectives.

This idea of the behaviour of people in organizations has persisted and gained strength, because it seems to explain many of the observable features of human behaviour. Yet McGregor contends that there are just as many facts which this view cannot explain. Why is it that examples can be found of higher productivity in units where control and coercion are minimal?

McGregor's answer is Theory Y which he claims is a more realistic explanation of human motivation and behaviour. Theory Y states that people are not by nature as Theory X supposes them to be, but they become so as a result of their treatment in organizations. In fact, work is as natural as play and rest. The average worker can learn to seek responsibility. There is, moreover, a great resource of self-direction, contribution to problem-solving and co-operative potential which is completely untapped. Management should make it possible for people in organizations to develop these characteristics in themselves. The organization should be such that people can realize their own potential by contributing to the achievement of organizational objectives.

McGregor, therefore, sees an effective organization as one which has replaced direction and control with integration and co-operation, and in which everyone affected by a decision can contribute to the making of the decision. The units of the organization are interacting groups of people who support each others' functions. 'Staff' is not the instrument of top management to control the line, but supplies a service to all levels for the furtherance of organizational objectives.

The ideal is attained when every member of the organization can identify himself with the objectives of the organization and feel that his contribution is worthwhile and valued by his superiors.

McGregor's views are typical of recent thinking among a group of modern psychologists and sociologists. They are founded on a vast amount of research by McGregor himself, and others, including Rensis Likert and Chris Argyris. These two have been singled out for discussion because, like McGregor, their writings contain several central concepts which are relevant to the study of organization.

Rensis Likert
Likert, another social psychologist, set up the Survey Research Centre, Michigan University. This later became the Institute for Social Research with Likert as its Director.

In his book *New Patterns of Management* Likert examines the managerial style of supervisors and the effects of different attitudes of supervisors on the productivity of those who work under them.

Many companies, he finds, encourage the use of the principles of scientific management. The job is broken down into its component parts and the best method of performing the job is developed. People are then recruited and trained to do the job, and supervisors are installed to see that the job is done in the specified way, at an acceptable rate. Research has shown that supervisors who operate against this background and share a belief in this philosophy of management tend to have charge over units with low productivity; 'that is, those supervisors whose units have a relatively poor production record tend to concentrate on keeping their subordinates busily engaged in going through a specified work cycle in a prescribed way and at a satisfactory rate as determined by time standards'. The emphasis of the supervisor's job is on getting the work done. Likert calls this orientation of supervision 'job-centred'.

In contrast, supervisors of high-producing units tend to be 'employee-centred'. They 'focus their primary attention on the human aspects of their subordinates' problems and on endeavouring to build effective work groups with high performance goals'. Under 'employee-centred' supervision, operatives are helped to do the job well for their own satisfaction as much as for the attainment of departmental goals. There is maximum participation in the setting of goals and making decisions; and more emphasis is placed on the achievement of goals than on the methods to be used.

Likert's ideal system of management is what he calls an 'interaction-influence system'. The most effective way of integrating the goals of work groups and organizational goals is by problem-sharing between superior and subordinate. Each supervisor and manager, therefore, should belong to two different levels; he should belong to a work group which includes his subordinates and a work group which includes his superior. In this way management should construct work groups, linking them into the organization by means of men who hold overlapping group membership. Effective groups and maximum participation by group members hold the key to effective organizational functioning.

For Likert, management is essentially a relative process. There are no general rules which can be applied to all situations. A manager must adapt his style to the group which he leads. One difficulty has been that a manager often cannot know whether he is on the right track,

58

because of inability to measure aspects of human behaviour. This is no longer completely the case: there are now a number of ways of trying to obtain measurements of such things as the level of motivation, the extent of group loyalty, the efficiency of communication. Such information will enable management to see where action needs to be taken, then, Likert says (borrowing from Follett), everyone can obey the 'law of the situation'. And, furthermore, the use of the law of the situation has greater power today than in Follett's day, since 'many variables . . . can be measured now . . . and can provide objective data where previously only impressions and judgements were available'.

Chris Argyris

Argyris is a social scientist and Professor of Industrial Administration at Yale University. Like the previous two writers he has concentrated on attempts to explain the behaviour of people in organizations. His books include *Personality and Organization, Understanding Organizational Behaviour*, and more recently *Integrating the Individual and the Organization*.

Argyris has developed as his main theme the thesis that formal organization requires 'behaviour that tends to frustrate, place in conflict, and create failure for, psychologically healthy individuals'.

There are a number of 'unintended consequences of the interaction' between the needs of individuals and the needs of the organization. Both sets of needs become adapted and frustrated, and an 'informal group organization' springs up, with norms appropriate to the frustrated and apathetic individuals who comprise it. Thus the behaviour of the total organization is a function of the interaction of the needs of individuals, the needs of informal groups and the needs of the organization.

Why does this happen and what are the 'unintended consequences'? An individual, says Argyris, develops along several lines. He goes from the passivity of infancy to the activity of adulthood; from the dependence of a child to the independence of a man. On each line of development he tries to attain maturity – the end of the line. And the end of the line is complete 'self-actualization'. Each man sets his own goals and strives to attain them, adapting to his environment in the process.

An organization too has goals, and the means for achieving these goals are often clearly prescribed. It will usually employ the principles of specialization, command, control and direction to further its ends and adapt to its environment. The organization too is, in a sense, involved in a process of self-actualization. Unfortunately, no attempt is made to integrate the individual and the organizational processes of self-actualization. The consequences are very often the exact opposite of what was intended. Specialization prevents self-actualization by concentrating on a narrow front. The chain of command means that active individuals striving for independence become passive and dependent on their leaders.

The results of these unintended consequences often appear in more concrete form. People may leave the organization or they may simply group together with others who feel equally apathetic. The latter happens most often and explains the obstructional elements in many organizations. And, unfortunately, the most common reaction from management is to increase the pressure; this only serves to increase the problem.

Argyris proposes some approaches to solving the problem. At a low level 'job enlargement' should be encouraged, giving the individual more opportunity to use his abilities. He should be allowed to participate in decisions affecting him. Budgets should not be imposed from above; better results can be achieved by prior consultation and acceptance. Every possible action should be taken to allow the individual to gain a greater control over his environment.

Even a passing acquaintance with an organizational atmosphere can show the frustrations and aggressions to which organizational life gives rise. The school of writers that includes McGregor, Likert and Argyris, took this common observation as their starting point and attempted to explain it. Until recently theirs was not a theory of organization but a collection of ideas about the causes and effects of malorganization. However, particularly in the past decade, research projects are revealing more constructive concepts which can be incorporated and given practical application in organization planning. In fact, no one concerned with organization planning can any longer justify an ignorance of the behaviour of people in organizations. Such is the impact of writers like McGregor, Likert and Argyris.

PART B

Theory

What is organization about? The sequence of chapters in Part B follows the chronological sequence of a practical reorganization of an enterprise, although the subjects are discussed mainly from a theoretical standpoint. The process of formal organization consists theoretically of four distinct stages: defining objectives, grouping activities, delegating authority to perform these activities, and specifying individual roles.

    Chapter 5 defines the purpose of a business organization and emphasizes the importance of objectives as the starting point of organization planning. Chapter 6 looks at the way activities, necessary to achieve objectives, can be grouped together. Chapter 7 considers the need to delegate activities and the accompanying problems of authority and responsibility. Finally, Chapter 8 examines the composition of jobs and the relationships of one job to another.

Chapter 5

The Purpose and Objectives of Organizations

Why have Objectives?

Any company which is to have a chance of being successful must know the areas in which it is most likely to find success. Where are we going? What is our business? What are our objectives? These are important questions for any company. They are important, in the first instance, because a company without aims cannot plan, and lack of planning makes development uncertain, to say the least. Secondly, without objectives a company has no sure way of measuring its performance and the soundness of its methods and structure. The company must identify its objectives, ask whether they are both worthwhile and attainable, then organize to achieve them.

The relationship between objectives and organization is not a new concept. Fayol wrote that management has to 'see that the human and material organization is consistent with the objectives, resources and requirements of the concern'. And Urwick said that 'the first thing you do when you look ahead is to try to provide the means, human and material, to meet the future situation which you foresee'.

However, until quite recently, writers tended to ignore the importance of objectives as vital links between the organization and its environment: they emphasized, rather, the internal significance of objectives to the organization. The comparison of organizational open systems with other types of open system has shown that an organization will not survive unless input, both human and material, is maintained. And this cannot happen, unless the environment, which supplies the input, is finding continuing satisfaction with the organization's output.

.   .   .

Primary Objectives – Survival, Profit and Growth

The search for a single, all-encompassing objective for business organizations has concerned, and often frustrated, many writers on management. The basic difficulty is that what seems at first sight to be an end,
can usually be viewed as simply a means to a more general, but less
obvious end. The company director whose first reaction is that he is in
business to make a profit, has an obligation to shareholders, feels a duty
to the community, to the employees, to his family, to himself.

The profit motive has been given a great deal of importance and
deserves further examination. No successful company can afford to
emphasize immediate short-term profit to the exclusion of all other
considerations. And no successful company does. If this were to
happen, research, product-innovation and capital investment would be
ignored. Everything possible would be done to cut costs and the
company's ability to satisfy the markets of the future would suffer.
Most successful companies have not been afraid to accept reduced
profits in the short-term to provide investment for the future.

In an attempt to resolve this argument we shall propose that the
overall objective of a business organization is to be successful. But at
best this is a rather intangible concept: to make it meaningful we must
define success. Most of the companies that are generally considered to be
successful have three factors in common: they survive, they make a
profit and they grow. By these three means they can give continuing
satisfaction to the major demands of those groups that have a stake in
the company. The continuance of this satisfaction is implicit in the
survival of the company: employees want a certain amount of security
of employment; suppliers want a reasonably stable market; shareholders
want some safety for their investment; the community as a whole has
a great interest in the continuing prosperity and employment provided
by the company; and finally, the market needs to find continuing
satisfaction with the company's products.

Shareholders also want to receive some return for their investment,
and employees some return for their labour; without profit neither is
satisfied for long. Top management wants growth to achieve greater
personal prestige and power; shareholders too want the capital gain which
growth in size brings. Only then by achieving these three, survival, profit and
growth, can a company satisfy those who have an interest in it. These
three, therefore, are the primary objectives of a business organization.

64

Whether the organization survives and grows to make a profit or makes a profit to survive and grow, is almost analogous to the question of 'which came first: the chicken or the egg?' The problem of priority between survival, growth and profit is as irrelevant to the study of business organization as the chicken-egg dilemma is to poultry farming.

However, although profit is proposed as an objective close to the top of the hierarchy of objectives, it is not suggested that managers should single-mindedly seek short-term maximum profit. Earlier we mentioned the detriment to the company's future that can result from attempts to maximize profits at any one time. Theorists may tell us that price less cost equals profit, but we all experience the difficulties of setting prices; we know that cost reduction must be exercised with future requirements in mind; and we realize that there is an element of risk involved in all our operations. As a result, we aim at a satisfactory level of profit, not the maximum. We set as our profit goal a target which will allow us to meet our commitments, economic and social, and ensure that we can continue to do so.

Secondary Objectives

Placing survival, growth and profit at the top of the hierarchy of objectives, we can propose as secondary objectives those which make a direct contribution to these three. Of first importance are the company's marketing objectives. We can define the function of marketing as 'ensuring that the resources of the company are used to design, produce and sell products in such a way as to win the maximum number of favourable buying decisions'. The marketing function, therefore, permeates every aspect of a successful business. It is essential, therefore, for a company to define its marketing objectives, to determine its markets, to decide on the means of satisfying those markets, and thus to make explicit the contribution of marketing to the survival, growth and profitability of the company.

Defining a market is never an easy matter, and many companies have been led to the brink of collapse by unenlightened definitions of their markets and the sort of business they were in. The Hollywood film industry and American railway companies are often quoted in this context. The fountain-pen manufacturers who have survived best after the introduction of ball-point pens have been those who carefully

65

examined their markets, and decided that they were, in fact, producing a gift rather than a writing instrument – a simple but vital difference of orientation.

This discussion of marketing objectives has led us naturally to the subject of product innovation. The need for new products in a rapidly changing environment does not need to be argued. In certain areas, however, less attention is given to innovation than is healthy for the future of the business. For example, no bank can ignore the need to create new services for investors and borrowers, and insurance companies should constantly be developing schemes to attract new customers. Nor should it be solely the function of research departments to innovate. We can innovate in the way we produce as well as in what we produce. We can innovate in our methods and procedures.

Innovations in methods and procedures should increase efficiency, and efficiency is itself an area in which objectives need to be stated. However, it is clearly not the sole objective, as was often implied in early management literature. To regard it as such is to equate efficiency with success. Efficiency simply introduces the concept of cost, and relates the achievement of objectives to the cost. But by virtue of its contribution to profit, objectives concerning efficiency should be defined.

Many other aspects of the business vitally affect the achievement of the overall objectives. We are here concerned with such activities as the acquisition of property, machines, men, material and money and their effective use. Unlike marketing, innovation and efficiency, which should concern every business enterprise about equally, these other aspects may vary in importance from company to company. This is not to say, however, that any one of them can be totally ignored by any company.

Objectives and Organization Structure
A great deal of attention has been given so far to the subject of objectives without relating it specifically to organization structure; but it is important to establish the need to define objectives on its own merits first. If we were to say simply that we must have objectives so that we know how to organize to achieve them (true though it may be) we would be greatly understating the case for objectives. Not only that, we would, in effect, be putting the cart before the horse, and tending

66

towards that insularity which views an organization as a machine, a closed system whose success is determined purely by its internal efficiency. Obviously the defined objectives will affect the organization structure, but we should not allow the process to be reciprocal; we must not define certain objectives simply because our present organization structure will help us achieve these objectives rather than other objectives which may make a greater contribution to success, though the time clearly will come when the investment in a particular structure is such that no change should be made until a sufficient return has been received from it.

What are likely to be the effects of objectives on organization structure? First, the definition of objectives will highlight the key functions of the business. There are obvious examples: the importance of advertising for mass consumer goods, the importance of product development in computers. A less obvious, but more poignant example is the case of Crown-Zellerbach, an American pulp and paper company. This company saw a long-term shortage of timber as a threat to its survival, and so established a 'long-range forest building' function which is planting the trees that the company will use fifty years from now. Again, successful companies in the 'rag-trade' have design as a key function.

Defining objectives, therefore, not only reveals the activities which an organization needs to perform, but will often show the relative importance of those activities. It will give an indication of the organizational level most appropriate for some functions, and the relationship between the functions. In the case of Crown-Zellerbach, it was clear that long-range forest building would have been neglected if it were not organized as a separate, major function.

A definition of objectives will also show the decisions that need to be made. And the extent of the contribution of decisions to achieving objectives will determine the level at which decisions must be made; similarly, the amount of harm to the achievement of objectives that any bad decision can do will determine how far down the chain of command it can be allowed to be made.

These definitions of key functions and decisions, resulting from the definition of objectives, provide a framework within which the detailed organization structure can be built.

It is not intended in this chapter to examine the setting of objectives

67

as a practical exercise, nor the problems of getting people to work for the organizational objectives. These subjects have their place in later chapters. There is, however, one further point which may touch on both these subjects and which must figure in any discussion of objectives. It is the question of how far we go in defining objectives. By this we mean two things: first, should objectives be set for every activity in an organization?; and second, how specific should an objective be?

Departmental Objectives

There are obvious advantages for a company in ensuring that even the smallest and least significant unit of its activities has objectives which make a contribution to the overall objectives; we might even extend this to individuals. Such a microscopic approach would highlight not only the extent and significance of the contribution of each unit or individual, but would thus give top management a guide to organization structure. It would show the relative importance of units and individuals; and the way in which unit objectives combined to contribute to overall objectives would indicate the primary relationships that have to be established between the units themselves. Furthermore, it is not uncommon for a company to find units which make no significant contribution, especially companies whose objectives are not under constant review.

In practice, however, the definition of unit objectives is fraught with difficulties. In a production department, where the output and contribution is tangible and can be measured, budgets, targets and objectives can be set in meaningful, operational terms. But in advertising, for example, or public relations, the effects of the activity are less direct. Indirect measurement is, however, possible, and new ways of overcoming this practical difficulty are constantly being developed.

The reaction of individuals to objectives will often provide greater difficulties. We owe to the researches of many psychologists the knowledge that people have their own objectives and that these may conflict with the objectives of the company. Where this happens, the contribution of the individuals and departments concerned will be diminished. Many departments in which conflict has been found and studied by researchers had what we might call 'unenlightened' managers, who imposed rigidly both objectives and methods of achieving the objectives

68

THE PURPOSE AND OBJECTIVES OF ORGANIZATIONS

on their subordinates. Most people do not enjoy working in a strait-jacket; they do enjoy increasing power over their environment. Securing co-operation in the achievement of company objectives means encouraging the integration of individual and organizational needs by allowing subordinates to share in setting objectives, to share in achieving objectives and to share the rewards of achieving objectives.

This does not in any way alter the importance, advantages, and principle of defining company objectives. The difficulty has been always in the practice not the principle.

Precision versus Vagueness in the Definition of Objectives

On the question of the preciseness of objectives we shall again look at the advantages first. The more specific an objective is, the less easily it is misunderstood, and the smaller the difficulty that is experienced in communicating it to others. Also the likelihood of conflict between objectives is reduced. A specific objective is a more meaningful criterion for judging performance.

All these are strong arguments for specific objectives. At departmental level and below they are particularly valid, and there is little quarrel with them apart from the practical difficulties indicated earlier. When we consider more comprehensive objectives, however, such as the overall company objectives in the areas of marketing and innovation, not only are there practical difficulties in being specific but there can be positive dangers. If we concentrate on too specific and narrow a field, an objective may have the very opposite effect by excluding from our focus both impending dangers and profitable opportunities. Opportunities are not discovered by 'ultra-purposeful action proceeding according to blueprint and schedule'.[1] Managers must be allowed to develop and use 'side-sight', otherwise the business may follow its straight and narrow path to collapse, by failing to adapt to a changing environment.

Summary

The primary objectives of a business organization are survival, growth and profit. To achieve these a company must define its secondary

[1] B. M. Gross, *The Managing of Organizations*.

objectives especially in the areas of marketing, innovation and efficiency. Because an organization is an open system, company objectives essentially describe the way in which the company intends to secure a continuing supply of human and material resources by its operations.

The objectives of a company will affect its organization structure by highlighting the key activities and decision areas. These will provide the skeleton of the structure.

There are great advantages to be gained by the setting of unit and individual objectives, but the individuals concerned must share in decisions which affect themselves. At unit and individual levels objectives can be defined as specifically as the nature of the activity and the wish to avoid stifling initiative allow. At the higher level of overall company objectives, especially in marketing and innovation, a broader view encourages top management's awareness and adaptability to a changing environment.

Chapter 6

Grouping Activities

Bases for Division

Effective business performance is that which achieves objectives which contribute to the survival and prosperity of the company. In both Chapter 2 and Chapter 5, the importance of objectives in determining the operations of the business was discussed. Also in Chapter 2 the principle of equifinality was mentioned. If we apply this principle to the organization of a company, we must conclude that there is more than one way to organize for effective business performance; and the diversity of modern company structures confirms this. One of the most specific and obvious differences is in the bases that different companies use for grouping their activities. In this chapter, it is intended to discuss the most commonly used bases for grouping activities, and to attempt to show the superiority of certain groupings. This will not contradict the principle of equifinality, since, although there may be many ways of reaching the same conclusion from a particular starting point, at a given time and in given circumstances, there are advantages, in such areas as efficiency or flexibility, in grouping activities in one way rather than another.

A company will often use a mixture of bases for grouping activities; for example, the sales department may be organized on a regional basis and the production department may be split into units making different products. Usually, however, a company has one basis for grouping which is predominant and which is reflected at the top of the organizational hierarchy. We can call this the main division of activities. And it is the basis on which a company makes this main division that we are primarily concerned with in this chapter.

Two such bases have already been mentioned, regional and product. Others which will be covered will include decisions and communications, function, customers, process and equipment.

Grouping Activities on the Basis of Region or Location

Many companies have, for a number of years, organized individual departments, such as sales, on a regional basis. The same type of organization is reflected in the basic subdivision of activities of a number of large, international companies. For example, one American oil company has this top management structure:

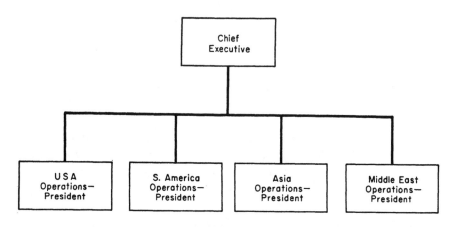

In some cases each regional division has complete autonomy in the major aspects of the business, such as production, sales and innovation.

Banking concerns too are normally organized on a regional basis. Although less autonomy is allowed, the basic activities of banking are performed within the local branches. It is difficult to see how any other basic structure would suit the needs of the bank. In examining the needs of banks, we will see quite clearly the advantages of regional organization. A bank must be fully conscious of its financial environment. The manager must know when his customers' businesses are doing well or about to go broke. He must keep informed and act on his information immediately.

Regional organization gives the opportunity for a more rapid collection and communication of information, and more speed and accuracy in reaction to local factors. Where these needs are supremely important, a company that is not organized on a regional basis, with each region having a large measure of autonomy, will find the achievement of objectives an uphill climb.

Grouping Activities on the Basis of the Market

Regional organization will in some companies mean the same thing as grouping on the basis of markets; for example, companies refer to their Home Sales Division catering for the Home Market, and European Sales Division catering for the European Market. Another definition of a market, however, is a group of people with similar needs, and as such a market will often cut across regional boundaries. This principle can be seen in motor manufacturing companies. Organization into domestic, haulage, agricultural and sport divisions is not uncommon, and allows each division to concentrate on the changing needs of its market, whether it be the family motorist, the haulier, the farmer or the motoring enthusiast.

There is also a trend (not yet necessarily reflected in top management structure) for companies owning a number of departmental stores to differentiate between their immediate markets in the lines sold in particular stores. In London there are obvious differences, in quality and price, between goods sold in different areas by stores that are part of the same group. As well as this attempt to cater for different tastes and incomes, at least two companies have separated off, almost as companies within companies, departments aimed specifically at the buying habits of the fashion-conscious teenager.

Organization primarily designed to exploit particular markets, defined not as regions but as groups of people with similar needs, has been evident for many years. A market-based organization can focus the attention of management at all levels on what is, in effect, a main source of the company's survival and prosperity.

Grouping Activities on the Basis of Products

To some extent we may have prejudiced the case for grouping on the basis of product. But a product-based organization does not necessarily imply a product-oriented company. A company with a market-oriented management has an equal chance of success whether it is organized on the basis of products or markets. For example, Imperial Chemical Industries divides its activities into such product groups as dye-stuffs, plastics, paints, man-made fibres, metals and alkali. The General Motors Corporation is organized at the operating level into six main groups, which include Car and Truck Group, Body and Assembly Group, Accessory Group and Engine Group.

There are, furthermore, a number of distinct advantages in grouping activities around products. A company can make best use of the specialized knowledge of its employees by allowing them to concentrate on a limited range of products to which their expertise is most applicable. The desire to do this has led in some office equipment companies to a distinction in operations between electro-mechanical and electronic machines. With a product-based organization structure each product or group of products gets attention, both in sales and production. More important, if organization is completely on a product basis, so that each product unit becomes a profit centre, the performance and potential of individual products (and managers) can be more easily calculated, and unprofitable lines (and ineffective managers) more clearly seen.

Similar to product-based grouping is the comparatively new technique of 'project management'. The aircraft and construction industries often organize a complete management structure around the demands of a new project. These particular industries have in common both time and cost problems. Their products are large and complex. Each new project requires the attention of every function of the business; the project must be financed, its market must be found, its costs controlled, it must be engineered and produced to meet specifications. With several projects 'on the boil' at the same time, it is likely that certain aspects of each would be neglected. To overcome this possibility, what amounts to a separate organization is formed for each project. Every demand of the project is catered for by having a complete management team whose objective is to develop the project into a profitable business enterprise. The advantages are clear: co-ordination on a project can more easily be achieved; team-spirit motivates those employed on the project since they can more easily identify themselves with the limited objectives of the project. An obvious disadvantage, however, is the possible insecurity felt by team members, who even upon successful completion of the project may find themselves without a job.

Despite this difficulty, however, there is every sign that project management, like product-based organization, will be used more widely. Both provide a solid foundation for determining accountability, and so are an ideal environment for decentralization which will be discussed in the next chapter.

Grouping Activities on the Basis of Functions

The main subdivision of activities most commonly found in companies throughout the world is based on the functions which those activities perform. A stereotype of these companies might look like this:

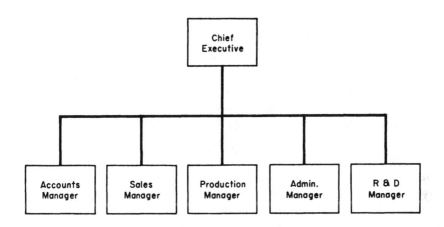

The main argument in favour of such a top management structure is on the face of it quite a strong one. It derives its origin from the principle of specialization. An accountant by focusing his attention on his own specialism and being allowed direct access to the head of the business has every opportunity to develop the accounting function to a very high level of performance. Similarly for sales, production, personnel, etc. Such an organization is also more likely to reap certain economies of scale. If accounting is centralized, fewer machines will be necessary than if each production unit has its own accounting department.

Organization based on function is, however, 'a second choice for any but the small enterprise'.[1] The disadvantages are numerous. First, just as grouping on the basis of products can simplify accountability, so grouping on the basis of function complicates it and makes performance more difficult to measure; the profitability criterion cannot be applied. Secondly, there is the problem of co-ordination at the top. Follett's remark has been quoted before and here it is particularly apt: 'Strand should weave with strand, and then we shall not have the clumsy task of trying to patch together finished webs.' The integration of functions to

[1] P. F. Drucker, *Practice of Management*.

75

achieve company objectives should start at the bottom of the organizational hierarchy and should be the responsibility of every level of supervision, not simply the man at the top. And what of this man at the top? In many cases, a company is asking a man with many years' experience of a specialist activity to abandon his specialism and become a generalist. He must give up his narrow expertise and his ingrained loyalties which the organization structure has encouraged him to develop, if he is not to find an 'outsider' being recruited in his place.

Every functional department forces its members to become introspective and narrow in their business horizons. It concentrates attention on professionalism and expertise, possibly to the exclusion of effective business performance. The desire of individuals for self-aggrandizement is satisfied by functional empire-building. The desire in itself can benefit a company, but not if it supplies the empire-builders with the tools of demolition rather than construction. Empire-builders should have their attention focused on markets, so that they become profit-builders.

It is tempting to dismiss the case for organization on the basis of function, especially when the arguments against it are so strong. Many companies, however, have organized in this way and been successful. How much more successful they would have been with a different structural basis we shall probably never know. It is likely, however, that up to a certain size, in mono-product companies with one clearly homogeneous and settled market, there are few alternatives to an organization based on function.

Grouping Activities on the Basis of Process or Equipment
Very rarely is a complete company organization structure based on a production process or the equipment used in the process. But quite often such an organization is evident within the production unit itself. In textiles, for example, there are usually different sections for spinning, weaving, dyeing, inspection and despatch. In the production of steel, the process does have a significant effect on the organization. Because of the need for continuous production, shifts have to be organized, each with its own management structure and service team.

Sheet metal-working departments are often organized on the basis of the different machines used; there will usually be a press section, drills section and lathe section. We are often reminded that it is more efficient to bring the machines to the work, but clearly in a company dealing with small batch metal-work, it is safer to secure the benefits of specialization. In such a company the structure might be a combination of machine-based and function-based groupings, like this:

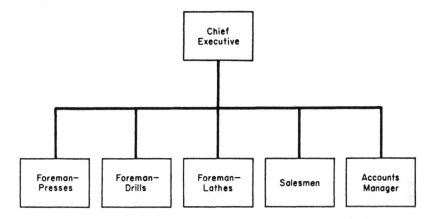

It is unlikely, however, that in companies of greater size the influence of the production machines or process will be very evident in the basic subdivision of activities.

Grouping Activities on the Basis of the Decisions that have to be made
There is a growing recognition of the importance of good information systems. Cybernetics, information theory and general systems theory all point to decision-making as a prime function of management. And with the greater use of computers some envisage the time when it will be almost the sole function of management.

For the present, the systems approach to organization takes as its starting point the decisions that have to be made to achieve company objectives. The main decision areas are listed and the information needed to make effective decisions is determined. The grouping of activities is then based on the need to minimize the time spent on communicating information. Where there is conflict between particular groupings, the question of how much speed is necessary in decision-making will determine the more beneficial arrangement.

In effect, this is little more than a different approach; the groupings established will often be the same as could be found by other approaches.

77

What it does, however, is encourage the management of a company to anticipate the need to make decisions, rather than have the need forced on them unprepared. Obviously, unexpected circumstances will still arise, but the more decisions a manager can anticipate, the more time he will have to deal with the unexpected. In any case, a check should always be made to ensure that a manager is not prevented from making a decision by lack of information.

Whatever basis is chosen for grouping activities, the final groupings should satisfy certain conditions. Firstly, each group must be 'manageable' – the limited supervisory capacity of individuals should be taken into account. This is the question of Span of Control. Secondly, the groupings should simplify rather than complicate the task of co-ordination. Thirdly, the basic structure should, as far as possible without conflicting with other desirable achievements, reap the benefits of economies of scale since this will contribute to profitability. And finally, the grouping should essentially further the attainment of company objectives.

Span of Control

It is not surprising that the Span of Control question has received a great deal of attention from writers on organization. Clearly the success of organization will depend, among other things, on the abilities of the people involved; and one consequence of this dependence is the need to avoid overburdening managers with supervisory responsibility. Hence the search for the magic number of subordinates that one man should be asked to supervise.

It may be felt, however, that the relevance of Span of Control to the exercise of grouping activities can be overstated. Classical writers implied that the need to limit the Span of Control of managers was almost the first consideration. On the contrary, no one would think of asking a marketing manager to supervise a production control section simply because the production manager already had too many supervisory duties. The bases for grouping are determined by other factors: the Span of Control 'principle' merely acts as a check to see whether the intended groupings are 'manageable'.

Viewed in this light, the Span of Control problem is very much a practical problem. Whether a particular grouping is 'manageable' depends not only on the number of subordinates that the manager of the grouping must supervise; the nature of the activities in the grouping, the co-operation among the subordinates, the abilities of the particular manager and many other factors affect the 'manageability' of groupings. Each one will have to be considered on its own merits.

The strongest arguments that have been advanced to support a limited Span of Control have a theoretical rather than a practical basis. The great popularity of statements of 'magic numbers' was boosted by the theoretical basis given by the French mathematician and consultant, Graicunas. The possible total number of 'relationships', according to Graicunas, can be found using the formula

$$ N \left\{ \frac{2^N}{2} + N - 1 \right\} $$

where N is the number of subordinates. According to this formula, where there are only two subordinates there could be six relationships; where there are eight subordinates, there could be as many as one thousand and eighty relationships, all of which could demand the attention of the supervisor. This formula is very theoretical, and treats the relationships as quantitative rather than qualitative.

The theory can also be criticized for ignoring the fact that the complexity of the supervisor's task varies with the organizational level. Even contemporaries of Graicunas noticed that a greater Span of Control would be possible at the lowest level of supervision. And Davis distinguished between 'the span of executive control' and the 'unit of supervision'. The former, he said, should be about five people, but the latter may range from ten to thirty.

Important though it may be to avoid overburdening the manager with supervisory duties, an over-emphasis on limiting his Span of Control can lead to worse consequences. Clearly the more we limit the Span of Control, the more we lengthen the chain of command and increase the number of organizational levels, with subsequent problems in communication and motivation. A decision made at the top takes longer to filter down to the bottom, and the likelihood of distortion *en route* is increased. The matrix of departmental objectives becomes more complex, and those at the lower levels have more difficulty in seeing the relevance of their efforts. Moreover, promotion comes in such small steps that it ceases to motivate. A flat structure with a minimum of levels has every advantage over the more common pyramidal structure in these respects. So the need to limit the Span of Control must be weighed carefully against the benefits of reducing the number of organizational levels.

We often hear the lament that particular managers cannot delegate. Usually it is a case of 'will not' rather than 'cannot'. They are afraid to manage by exception, and will not resist the temptation to check up. For such a manager, increasing the Span of Control might bring positive benefits in the form of increased effectiveness. His men would merely 'report' to him rather than be 'supervised' by him.

No one would deny that the supervisory capacities of individuals are limited. It is, however, important to realize the consequences of over-emphasizing the matter, and to appreciate the benefits that can be gained by increasing rather than restricting the Span of Control. It now seems amazing that classic writers should have tried to give a general formula for the Span of Control when it so obviously depends on the particular circumstances.

What are the relevant factors in determining the Span of Control? Firstly, the ability of the manager and the amount of work other than supervision that he has to do. It is often overlooked that supervision is only part of a manager's total function. (One survey[1] showed it to be about one-third.) If we increase the number of his subordinates, therefore, his work load increases, but not in the same proportion.

Secondly, Span of Control will be affected by the supervisory needs of the subordinates. These, in turn, depend on the competence of subordinates, whether they form a co-operating rather than a conflicting work group, and how much their jobs have been simplified by a good information system and routine decision-making. (For example, A. K. Rice[2] claims to have found large Spans of Control in industries where the technology has more built-in controls.) Moreover, where the jobs of subordinates are very similar, their supervisory needs also will be similar, and so they will make smaller demands on the supervisor's time. Finally, personal assistants can be used to relieve managers of specified duties.

[1] G. Copeman, *How the Executive Spends his Time.*
[2] *The Enterprise and its Environment.*

Each case, therefore, should receive separate consideration. This may not be as helpful as the prescription of an upper limit for the Span of Control; yet it is far less likely to mislead.

Co-ordination

We have already mentioned the difficulties of co-ordination, if it is viewed as the responsibility of top management only. It should be far simpler to integrate activities at the lower organizational levels. Every supervisor should be encouraged to realize that although he may achieve the objectives of his unit without outside help, his achievement will contribute nothing unless it combines with the achievements of other units to reach higher-level objectives. The hierarchy of objectives, therefore, holds the key to organization for ease of co-ordination. The need to co-operate should be made explicit in the statements of departmental objectives. The essential linking for departmental activities should be demonstrated to every member of the department. A progress clerk should realize that his contacts with purchasing, production and marketing personnel are vital for improving customer service, thereby increasing market standing, which in turn contributes directly to the survival and prosperity of the business. A necessary precondition for co-ordination is the involvement of people in working for the right objectives, and realizing the value of their contribution.

A further essential condition is good communication. Project management developed out of the realization that where speed and accuracy of communication were important, grouping based purely on functions (production, selling, accounting, etc.) left much to be desired.

Co-ordination, it has been found, is more easily achieved on projects when the decisions to be made are analysed and the structure of the project team designed to speed communication of information. In any case, it is certain that where information needs are ignored, everyone is free to use his own methods and practices, to set his own objectives and pace. Synchronization and proper co-ordination in these circumstances are impossible.

It is not suggested that the grouping of activities should be designed merely to facilitate co-ordination. But it is, like the Span of Control, another factor to be taken into consideration. The Span of Control, we have implied, should be regarded merely as a check on the

81

practicability of groupings; on the other hand, the need for co-ordination should come into play earlier and should influence significantly the grouping of activities.

Economies of Scale

When discussing function as a basis for grouping activities, we touched on the economies that can be made by the centralization of equipment. This is only one of a number of ways in which a company can reap economies by larger scale or more specialized operations. The economist, E. A. G. Robinson,[1] stated five areas in which such economies could be achieved.

'Technical economies' come from the centralization of machines. To achieve these all clerical work connected with accounting might be grouped together; or a production unit might have separate sections for different types of equipment. In the 1950s it was felt that the computer would lead to rapidly increasing centralization, but, although a computer may handle work previously carried out by several departments, often these departments have retained their separate identity, with the computer acting in a service capacity.

'Managerial economies' can be obtained by allowing employees to specialize in activities most suited to their particular expertise. This can have two consequences, one beneficial, the other possibly dangerous. If it means grouping on the basis of a particular market or product to make use of the employees' expertise in that market or product, it is very likely to increase the effectiveness of the structure. If, on the other hand, men are to be allowed to specialize in a particular function, it encourages them to become myopic, and has all the other faults of function-based grouping.

'Financial economies' result from centralizing the company's activities concerning the acquisition of finance. The importance of the benefits to be gained in this area is seen in the fact that many companies, whose structures are in most respects highly decentralized, retain financial acquisition as a separate, centralized function, hoping thus to influence the size of loans and the rate of interest. The benefits of centralized buying too would come under this heading, with the advantages of securing quantity discounts and ensuring better quality and service.

[1] *The Structure of Competitive Industry.*

82

'Marketing economies' can be obtained by centralization. It may be possible to reduce the number of salesmen, to cut down transportation costs by rationalizing distribution, etc. On the other hand, certain product lines may be neglected, since salesmen may tend to concentrate on the easier selling lines to the detriment of the more profitable ones; and the unprofitable lines continue to be produced and reduce the overall profitability of the company because their effects are not immediately apparent.

Finally, there are 'risk-spreading economies'. Holding companies are examples of how investment can be designed to reduce the risk of overall loss.

It is the desire to gain full benefit from these economies that has led many companies to organize on a functional basis – often with disappointing results. It may be easy to measure the reduction in cost of centralized accounting, buying or selling, but it is difficult to gauge the relative continuing contribution of such departments to overall profitability. Moreover, there are some indications that increased size over a certain level may bring 'diseconomies' rather than benefits. It is safer, therefore, to regard economies of scale as secondary considerations, to be sought after only if they do not conflict with other more desirable aims of grouping activities, such as the need to achieve objectives and measure the contribution to this end of individual departments.

Size and Accountability

This discussion of economies of large-scale operations raises the whole question of size. Far from reaping benefits as a result of increased size, many of the larger British companies are not as profitable as the smaller ones. For example, in *Management Today* (September 1967), C. Pratten presented a table about which he concludes that 'the overall impression given is that the smaller companies tend to have the highest returns on gross assets'. In the chemical industry, for instance, companies in the £½m to £1m net assets range had a return on capital of 18·1 per cent, while those in the £100m and over range managed only 12·7 per cent.

However, in the United States, the same pattern is not discernible. What are the differences between the larger American companies and their British counterparts that account for this difference in levels of success? The basic advantage that most large American companies appear to have is a superior system of accountability. They have been able to preserve or create the small profit-centre which has a direct effect on the profitability of the smaller company. They have been able to set, for each significant unit of their operation, a target and to make the manager of that unit accountable for the capital assets he controls. They have been able to extend their systems of accountability down to the lowest levels and smallest units in the organization, so that each individual can see more clearly how his performance directly affects the profitability of the organization as a whole. In effect, they have preserved the ease of accountability in the small company while reaping the benefits conferred by financial strength in the large company.

Size on its own would appear to be of little benefit, but the large organization composed of small profit-accountable units may be the answer. We will return to this subject again in the next chapter when discussing decentralization.

Grouping to achieve Objectives

We shall end this chapter as we began it on the theme of organizing to achieve objectives. It is fitting that this should be so, because objectives are both the stimulus for organizing at all and the end to which organization structures should contribute.

The increasing popularity of organization based on product groups or markets, and of the project management type of structure, is not the result merely of fashion. Such structures have proved that success comes not simply from organizing to achieve efficiency of operation, but by directing attention at the achievement of objectives and the need to measure the extent of that achievement. If efficiency of operation facilitates or enhances this so much the better.

Summary

Activities have been grouped on many different bases. Although all such bases have advantages and disadvantages, in given circumstances one is likely to be more suitable than the others, though not for all time.

Grouping on the basis of region has an advantage where speed of reaction to local factors is important. Market-based grouping concentrates attention on the source of the company's future existence. Product-based grouping simplifies accountability and so encourages decentralization. Grouping by function allows personnel to reach a 'high' (but, perhaps, immeasurable) level of performance by specialization; it also provides the benefits of economies of scale. Grouping by process or equipment may benefit small companies and departments within larger companies, again through economies of scale. Grouping based on the decisions to be made will ensure that communication channels facilitate the flow of information and so improve co-ordination.

The Span of Control 'principle' should be used as a check on the 'manageability' of the groupings chosen. The actual Span of Control depends on the ability of the manager, the competence of and extent of co-operation between the subordinates, the nature of and similarity between the subordinates' activities, the amount of non-supervisory work which the manager must do, and his use of personal assistants. There must be balance between the Span of Control and the number of organizational levels.

Co-ordination should be based on the hierarchy of objectives. Members of the organization should realize that activities must be interrelated to achieve objectives. Co-ordination should start at the bottom. Good communication channels are essential to co-ordination.

Economies of scale may be 'technical', 'managerial', 'financial', 'marketing' or 'risk-spreading'. They should be pursued as long as they enhance the achievement of objectives. Size of itself, however, may actually bring about diseconomies of scale.

Delegation

In a Utopian society everyone would, by nature, work in harmony to achieve goals of benefit to all. No task would be overlooked, nothing would be duplicated. Each part would fit naturally into a scheme with every other part. Every man would realize his skills and his limitations. He would know by instinct the part he must play, and why he, rather than any other, was suited to that part.

In the real world things are very different. In our attempts to approximate to the ideal we need education, motivation and prohibition. Although grouping together is natural, a group achieves little unless the individuals who comprise it are encouraged to realize, accept and perform their respective roles. These are, therefore, the three requirements: people should be conscious of the results they have to achieve; they should feel a desire to achieve them; they should have the facilities, power and ability necessary to achieve them.

When the subject of delegation in enterprises is being discussed, the conversation too often takes the line that authority and responsibility can be tied up in neat packages and transferred from person to person at will. This cannot be so when both depend to such a large extent on the 'receivers' rather than the 'givers'.

In this chapter, an attempt will be made to show that effective delegation leans heavily on the three requirements mentioned above: the knowledge of what is to be achieved, the desire, and the facilities, power and abilities to achieve. This will involve a re-examination of the concepts of authority and responsibility.

When we have established what delegation means and what should be delegated, we can examine the problems to which delegation provides a solution, the advantages to be gained from delegation, and the factors affecting the extent of delegation. This will lead on to a discussion of centralization and decentralization.

The Nature of Authority

It has often been said that authority is an attribute of the job and not of the man. But if this is the whole truth, why is it that one man has more success in a particular job or position than another, when both by definition have the same amount of authority? A bus conductress has authority to ask a drunken passenger to get off the bus; she has such authority by virtue of her job. A bus conductor performs the same job and, therefore, should have the same authority, but the chances are that the inebriated passenger will take his leave more quickly.

Fayol defined authority as 'the right to give orders and exact obedience'. He called this official authority, but he also recognized that official authority by itself was often ineffective. Official authority was vested in the job rather than the person, but was enhanced by personal authority 'compounded of intelligence, experience, moral worth, ability to lead, etc. . . . '

The sources of formal or official authority are usually considered to be the institutions of society, especially the institution of private property. The shareholders of a company have a right to deal with their property (shares) as they see fit. They have the right to appoint others to administer their interests. Those they appoint assume some of the rights of owners by virtue of their appointment. One of these rights is the appointment of numbers of assistants to help them perform their task. Each assistant, therefore, assumes some part, however small, of the owner's rights, again by virtue of his appointment. In theory, therefore, a man has sufficient authority when he is not prevented by formal restrictions from performing the job for which he was appointed.

In fact even this measure of authority may be ineffective, unless a man has personal authority. The sources of personal authority are numerous. Examples of individuals who rely purely on charisma are not easily found in modern business. Perhaps the nearest approximation is the leader of an unofficial strike; certainly he has no formal authority, nor is his influence always the result of superior knowledge, experience or ability. Personal authority may also derive from the possession of information, an accumulated knowledge of facts; this

87

source of personal authority has recently acquired the name 'sapiential authority'. Then again, educational backgrounds, cultural environment, experience, all play a part in determining the personal authority that an individual will bring to a job.

When an executive is being recruited, these are among the many characteristics that will be examined. Most often the prospective superior will conduct at least one interview, if not the whole selection process. He will be looking for the qualities which he thinks will enhance the formal authority of the position. But very rarely are qualities specifically sought which would make a man acceptable to a particular group of subordinates, and never will subordinates interview a prospective superior.

Some writers have taken this point further. Simon[1] states that 'actual' authority, as opposed to formal authority, is measured by the extent to which one person can guide the behaviour of others without his guidance being questioned. This means that authority is the ability to make decisions that are obeyed without question. The person receiving the orders weighs the consequences of obeying or refusing to obey, and so has a considerable effect on the outcome of a particular situation.

The superior's job is to influence his subordinates to help them make better decisions, rather than to give orders without first creating a climate of acceptance. Delegation of formal authority to an individual is pointless unless that individual's leadership is accepted by his subordinates.

The concept of 'actual' authority as the ability to give orders which are obeyed without question derives strong support not only from many organization theorists, but from practice. We know that people without a measure of acceptance by those they lead, however great their formal authority, will only succeed in a totalitarian environment. On the other hand, the leaders of slave revolts have shown that success, in some cases complete, can be achieved without any formal authority derived from the institution of private property. Leaders of slave revolts rely on their personal strengths, and their leadership depends on their acceptance by their followers.

To return to the business organization, when a man is appointed to do a particular job, he expects there to be a formal authority structure. He expects his boss to be permitted to exercise a wider influence than

[1] *Administrative Behaviour.*

he himself may. He expects formal authority and he accepts the need for it. What he may decide to object to is the particular way in which authority is exercised over him. So it is the effectiveness of authority which depends on the receiver, rather than authority itself.

What are the consequences of this for delegation? Clearly the problem of obtaining a satisfactory performance from a supervisor is not solved simply by giving him certain formal powers. These can be delegated but they do not ensure success. The effectiveness of a supervisor is more or less than his formal authority, depending on the degree of acceptance his leadership finds among his subordinates. This cannot be delegated but is more fundamental to success. It is a human problem which will be discussed more extensively in Chapter 10.

The Nature of Responsibility

There are almost as many definitions of responsibility as there are management writers. Most of them, however, are specific statements of two general concepts of responsibility. Either responsibility is an obligation to perform a task, or it is the task itself. The former definition hangs on the Latin derivation of the word responsibility. It implies that a man who accepts a task can and should be held to account for the performance of that task; he must 'make a reply' either in the form of successful performance, or with reasons why success was not achieved. The second definition seems to derive its validity from the common practice of referring to the tasks a man should perform as 'his responsibilities'.

The question whether responsibility can be delegated can be answered differently for either definition. One man can pass to another the instruction to perform a certain task. But by doing so he does not absolve himself of any obligation he undertook, nor does he automatically create an obligation to himself on the part of his subordinate, unless that subordinate feels a need to perform the task. Responsibilities, in the sense of obligations, are not passed down the organization; rather, new responsibilities must be created at each level. A board of directors does not transfer its obligations (to shareholders) by appointing a general manager; it tries to create a new set of obligations to itself. Responsibility in this sense cannot be delegated, but the performance of a task can.

Much argument on this subject has concerned the extent to which the responsibilities (in the loose sense) can and should be defined. Clearly the form in which such 'responsibilities' are delegated, whether they are simply statements of results to be achieved, or minutely detailed prescriptions of methods, routines and procedures, may influence the performance of the individuals whose 'responsibilities' they are.

Most of the classical organization theorists advocate clear definitions of responsibilities. For example, Brech says: 'Long experience with problems of organization has made it ... abundantly clear that frictions and difficulties as to respective responsibilities arise only where responsibilities are not clear because they have never been written down. . . .'[1] Such writing down will help to avoid confusion, omission and duplication. It may also be used for other purposes, such as a basis for equitable remuneration and salary comparisons. It is further argued that a man whose duties have been clearly defined knows where he stands and has no fear of being held to account for a responsibility he was not aware of. He can proceed with his job free from the 'interference' of supervisors, since how can he go wrong when everything is so clearly defined?

It is unlikely, however, that at any but the lowest levels in an organization can these advantages be obtained by clearly defining and writing down a man's responsibilities. Let us consider the other extreme for a moment. Franklin D. Roosevelt we are told[2] purposefully avoided defining the 'responsibilities' of his staff: the disputes which inevitably arose had to come to him to be resolved; so he could keep his finger on the pulse of affairs, and more easily control a group of powerful and ambitious individuals. A recent development in business organizations has been an interest in 'free form'. A good example of 'free form' is the Litton Industries. In Litton there is no written organization chart, no written definitions of functions, no written plan, but everyone knows what the structure is and every manager has a plan in his mind.

The Litton Philosophy is certainly extreme and may not be effective in other organizations or at other times. A compromise seems to be the answer, but a compromise which incorporates the best of the extreme viewpoints. Managers should know what their function is,

[1] *Organization: The Framework of Management.*
[2] Schlesinger, *The Coming of the New Deal.*

the results that are expected and, in broad terms, the company philosophy about the means of achieving the results. They should realize the contribution they can and should make to the company's success. They should be aware of the relationship of their own responsibilities to the responsibilities of others. The emphasis should be on objectives and contribution, rather than mechanics. This will have the advantages of avoiding omission, duplication and general confusion, making the man aware of the results he is being asked to feel responsible for, and showing the relative importance of his position; it will avoid the narrowing of horizons with the inevitable loss of opportunities that over-definition can bring.

Some writers[1] have shown a more serious difficulty in the definition of individual responsibilities and the assessment of individual performance. They claim that if individual objectives are over-emphasized, this will lead to competition rather than co-operation. Individual assessment should only be used where the work is independent. In its place, group assessment is proposed. It is felt that a team with a particular aim will exert its own pressures on individuals within the team to conform and strive to achieve their aim.

The idea, however, may raise more problems than it solves. The point was made earlier that some delineation of responsibilities is necessary to avoid confusion. Furthermore, it is an accepted fact that people improve their performance more quickly and surely when they are given knowledge of their results. There is also evidence to show that for most tasks the ideal learning situation involves one teacher and one pupil. If a team fails, has every team member failed? Presumably we must believe so, but will those who feel they have performed as well as they could accept a share of the blame?

Competition within an organization is not harmful in itself. It can become so if it is allowed to direct performance to the wrong ends. If an organization structure is based on function, co-operation is cetainly more essential than competition and individual inter-function strife. If, however, each unit of the company is a separate product division, competition among unit-heads will often benefit the company as a whole.

Let us now try to summarize the components of successful delegation. The things that we can delegate are the performance of certain

[1] See for example Likert, *New Patterns of Management*, pp. 108 f.

tasks (responsibilities) and a measure of freedom of operation to carry out those tasks (formal authority). At the same time we must try to create an obligation (responsibility) to ourselves for the performance of the tasks. The man to whom we delegate and whom we try to obligate should have the qualities of intelligence, moral worth, knowledge, experience, etc. (personal authority) such that his *subordinates* will accept his leadership without question (actual authority).

What is to be Gained from Delegation?

There is a tendency to regard delegation as something that is always forced on a company owner by the pressure and volume of work. This idea originated from the treatment of organization as a problem of growth. The view was that delegation should be delayed as long as possible but that it was inevitable as time passed. This is to regard delegation purely as a defence mechanism, and to ignore the benefits of 'aggressive delegation'.

Delegation because of size can be either defensive or aggressive. The company owner, who finds his tasks have become too varied, too time-consuming or just too much for one man, will delegate certain of his tasks to assistants. On the other hand, a comparatively small company may be divided into divisions and almost complete autonomy given to division heads, not because the owner could not cope, but to create a more thrustful and competitive organization.

A particular function may be delegated so that it gets individual and constant attention. From a defensive angle, this often happens when a company has been started up around a particular product; the owner has the ideas and the technical know-how, but because of his interests in these areas insufficient time is spent on selling, and so he is forced to delegate. On the other hand, improvement of R & D may be delegated to one man, not because no one can find time for it with his present job, but because it is seen as a vital source of the company's future prosperity.

Perhaps the best example of aggressive delegation is delegation to exploit the advantages of a particular region or market. Again, this can be forced on a company, but a progressive and thrustful company will be at least one jump ahead of the pressures. Similar is the case of the successful company which is acquired by a larger concern. A
92

defensive attitude would be to incorporate the new company within the existing framework, when greater benefit might well accrue from allowing the existing management roughly the same amount of autonomy as they enjoyed previously.

Many of the recent arguments about the need for and advantages of more delegation have concentrated on decision-making needs and information theory. It is often stated that decision-making is the major part of a manager's function. An improvement in effectiveness of a manager's decisions contributes directly to the overall effectiveness of a company. It can be shown that the effectiveness of a decision decreases, the further away from the point of action it is made, and the longer the distance that the vital information must travel. In other words, if the information source and the point of action are fixed, the effectiveness of a decision depends on it being made by the person with the most direct access to both information and implementation channels relevant to that decision. Delegation of any decision-making task, therefore, should be to the person in such a position.

Once again this can be forced upon a company by the accumulation of unresolved problems at the top and the inevitable distortion of orders transmitted over a long distance and passed on by many people. Or it can be a step taken to capitalize on the often under-estimated decision-making ability of less senior executives, and so reap the benefits of speed and accuracy.

The Extent of Delegation
In discussing the delegation of decision-making, we have already touched upon the question: how far can I delegate? Obviously the gains from greater delegation must be weighed against the risks involved.

The simplest type of delegation and that which in most cases is a very early step in the life of a business, is delegation of formal authority to carry out an operation on behalf of the business. This occurs when the owner of a one-man business first employs operators. But even here there may be problems: does the operator have the formal authority to change his method of working? Does he set his own pace? And the higher we go in the organization, the more complex the problem becomes. To say, for example, that a man has charge over production tells us very little of the decisions he is formally authorized to

93

make. Does he make production control decisions? Can he buy new machinery? If so, how much can he spend?

If speed were the only consideration, we should delegate decision-making to the man who has quickest access to all relevant information. But decisions when made have to be acted upon, and the man who is nearest to the sources of information may not be the best one to implement a decision, even if he is qualified to make it. Conversely, many writers have argued that decision-making should be delegated as close to the scene of action as possible. And this has the advantage, in theory at least, that most of the information too will often be at the scene of action. It has the disadvantage that a weak executive closest to the scene of action, may be so involved in routine matters that he may not feel pressures nor see opportunities.

The results that are expected of a man should have the greatest effect on the amount of formal authority that is delegated to him. Fayol said that authority should be commensurate with responsibility, and many others have agreed. A man should not be held to account for something over which he had no formal authority, and to control the exercise of formal authority a man should be answerable for his actions. But Fayol is at least guilty of over-statement, like many prophets and pioneers. If the idea is applied too rigidly it has a number of undesirable consequences. First, if a man is to be held to account only for the things over which he has direct control, he is encouraged to look elsewhere for excuses for failure and to protect his own self-interests against the organization. It will tend to narrow his vision and he will be fearful of looking for opportunities which may benefit the company but which are outside his own sphere of activities. The view also tends to ignore the importance of personal authority, of the achievements of influence, and persuasion.

Fayol himself realized what is perhaps the greatest difficulty, that of measurement. He said, 'It is increasingly difficult to isolate the share of the initial act of authority in the ultimate result and to establish the degree of responsibility of the manager. The measurement of this responsibility and its equivalent in material terms evades all calculation.' Many attempts have been made to quantify and so control the amount of formal authority given. One example has been the idea of 'authority to commit', that is, to spend the company's money. But this is only relevant to part of the total decision-making task of a company.

Fayol saw the equation of authority and responsibility as a solution to a practical problem: the natural tendency of people to seek authority and avoid responsibility. People like McGregor would no longer accept the latter as the natural tendency of most people. But despite these criticisms, there is still some truth in Fayol's words. It is wrong to expect certain results from a man, when the restrictions imposed on him provide obstacles to the achievement of those results. It would be a useful, and perhaps enlightening, exercise for many companies to examine the extent of formal authority necessary for their executives to achieve the results expected. It might well lead to a redistribution of tasks, if it were found, for example, that a subordinate needs more formal authority than his boss.

In many companies, fear prevents managers from gaining full benefit from delegation. Since responsibility, in the true sense of obligation, cannot be passed on and the delegator is not absolved from his own obligation, he is afraid to commit to others tasks for which he will be held to account. The problem is difficult to overcome completely, but use of the technique of 'over-ride' may improve the situation. 'Over-ride' is analogous to the relationship between the real pilot and the automatic pilot on an aeroplane. The automatic pilot guides the plane towards its destination, making adjustments as necessary. In a sense, it is in control of the plane but the human pilot can take over (over-ride) at any time. If he does so too frequently, he loses the advantage of having an automatic pilot. If he becomes negligent of his over-riding responsibility, then the plane may be in danger.

In management, 'over-ride' is the concept of a higher, latent formal authority. It is not the same as management by exception, where normally the occasions for reference to higher management are pre-set. With 'over-ride' lower management may not have brought a particular matter to the attention of higher management. 'Over-ride' enables the delegator to be freed of detailed considerations while retaining ultimate control.

As a general rule, it will benefit the organization to have decision-making pushed as far down the chain of command as the situation will allow. And by the situation we mean: first, the competence of subordinates; second, the information available to the decision-maker; and third, the 'keyness' or scope of impact on the organization as a whole of the decision. These will provide the brake. The confidence of higher management, the desire for more effective decisions and operations must provide the impetus.

Centralization and Decentralization

A medium-sized company had five production units scattered throughout the country. Each production manager had an output target, a budget and a limit on capital expenditure, all determined without consultation by head office. The sales organization was based on ten regional offices. Each regional sales manager had a territory target, and a sales budget set by head office. All recruitment, R & D, accounting, labour relations and determination of methods and procedures were head office functions. The chairman was proud of his 'decentralized organization'.

There is a distinct difference, however, between physical dispersion and managerial decentralization. The latter implies primarily the delegation of formal authority, the pushing of decision-making down the chain of command.

Decentralization is the tendency to delegate formal authority to lower organizational units, and centralization the tendency to withhold such authority. Most companies are on a continuum between the two extremes. They are not alternatives: a company is not either centralized or decentralized; it is either more centralized or more decentralized. The extent of decentralization is reflected in the delegation of decision-making. A company is more decentralized the more that decisions are made at lower organizational levels and the more important those decisions are.

Greater decentralization has advantages, especially in the improvement of performance of managers. Middle and lower management have more job interest. The results for which managers can be held to account are more easily determined. Weak managers cannot hide, and good, young managers can be tested more realistically. The company can obtain greater flexibility and become more thrustful. There can be a quicker response to environmental factors when decisions are made where and when the need arises, rather than waiting for head office approval.

Some tasks, however, cannot be decentralized. Because of the importance of unions, one division of a company cannot be allowed to make decisions on the wages and conditions of employment which may affect the whole company. Such decisions are normally reserved for a centralized negotiating body. Again, most companies would be wrong to decentralize the function of acquiring finance.

Against the advantages of decentralization must be weighed the possible losses. Most obvious of the advantages which may be lost are the economies of large-scale unit-operating. But, however desirable such economies, they must never be allowed to have the force of a veto but must be kept in perspective. It is of little use having an inexpensive machine which produces unsatisfactory results.

A further argument put forward against decentralization is that each unit of a company will attempt to optimize its performance at the expense of the other units. The element of competition has been considered earlier. There is no harm in inter-unit rivalry if it is directed towards more effective business performance rather than simply towards greater recognition of a particular expertise. To have two product divisions competing for a market, in certain circumstances should be encouraged; but to have production and sales fighting each other to gain the favour of the Managing Director should be avoided in any circumstances.

The strongest argument against decentralization is the possible lack of uniformity and the lowering of standards in decision-making. But even this difficulty can be overcome by training, and by allowing junior managers to make decisions while exercising ultimate control through 'over-ride'.

The word decentralization may unfortunately imply a weakening of the centre of an organization. This is not the case; decentralization can strengthen the central authority, not by an increase in its powers but by a clarification of the part it should play. The head office of a more decentralized company should have a dual function, both 'line' and 'staff'. It is 'line' in the sense that it must knit together a highly individual top team; and it is 'staff' because it should help managers with technical aid to become more effective. It sets overall goals and checks goal-attainment, and reserves to itself certain duties which have an impact on the whole organization.

'Divisionalization' and 'Departmentalization'

In a number of places throughout this and previous chapters we have mentioned product-based and function-based organization. At this

97

stage it will be helpful to summarize and draw together these references. This is especially relevant at this time since product-based organization, though not a recent innovation, is gaining increasing popularity with organization planners.

Drucker seems to have been the first to distinguish clearly between the two, calling one Federal, the other Functional decentralization. Federal decentralization is based on product division; the basis of Functional decentralization is reflected in the name. More recently, and certainly more commonly in this country, the Federal type has been referred to as 'divisionalization'; and an apt title for its alternative is 'departmentalization'.

Both, therefore, are methods of decentralizing, and like centralization and decentralization can be considered as points on a continuum, like this:

Functionalized highly centralized companies	Integrated, departmentalized companies	Divisionalized companies	Conglomerates	Holding companies

(A conglomerate refers to a company whose products bear no obvious relationship to one another.)

Divisionalization itself is the organization of a company into virtually autonomous product groups. Divisionalization is particularly relevant where production technologies for the products differ. This will entail no loss of economies of scale in production, and divisions will not be interdependent. It is also a help, but not essential, if there are distinct markets for each product. Finally, each division should be large enough to sustain a full management team. Absolute size is not, however, a relevant factor: Sears, Roebuck have stores with as few as fifty personnel; at the other end of the scale the number employed in a General Motors division may be over 20,000.

The qualities which make divisionalization superior and departmentalization only a second choice have all been mentioned earlier, in this and the previous chapter. Recapitulating, divisionalization:

– concentrates attention on business performance

– makes management accountability clearer, so uncovering bad management and encouraging good management

- gives opportunities for testing tomorrow's top management under realistic conditions

- eases the task of co-ordination at the top

- encourages empire-builders to become profit-builders.

It cannot however be over-emphasized that successful divisionalization presupposes strong central guidance. Some tasks cannot be decentralized in certain circumstances. The following tasks should not be decentralized in any circumstances: the setting of overall company objectives, the planning of the organization structure, the selection of top central and divisional executives, the outlining of the values, philosophies and outlook of the company, the evaluation of the total business in relation to its overall objectives, and the retention and allocation of profits. These functions, at least, require company-wide co-ordination, and so need to be centralized.

Summary

Delegation involves transferring to others the formal right to perform certain tasks, and the attempt to create an obligation on the part of the person receiving that right to perform the task to a certain standard. To do this, the man must also have the qualities of intelligence, moral worth, knowledge, experience, etc., such that his subordinates will accept his leadership without question.

Delegation can be viewed both as a defence mechanism to alleviate pressure on overburdened top management, and as an aggressive move to secure the benefits of direct and immediate decision-making.

Greatest advantage can be gained by delegating as far as the competence of subordinates, the information available and the scope of impact of decisions will allow. Fear of delegation is caused by the fact that the delegator is still ultimately responsible. The problem can often be overcome by using the technique of 'over-ride'.

Managerial decentralization implies the tendency to delegate formal authority; managerial centralization the tendency to withhold it. The extent of decentralization is, therefore, measured by the number and scope of decisions made at lower organizational levels. The advantages of decentralization are similar to those of delegation: more immediacy in decision-making, greater organizational flexibility and drive, and more job interest for junior and middle management. The disadvantages of decentralization are not, in most cases, as serious as is often believed; but there are certainly a number of tasks which cannot be decentralized.

Decentralization may be product- or function-based. The former, known as divisionalization, is to be preferred, especially where product technologies and markets are 'discrete', and the individual divisions are large enough to support a full management team. Again there will be certain tasks which require company-wide co-ordination and which must, therefore, be centralized.

Chapter 8

Roles

The most common dictionary definition of the word 'role' is the activities which an individual is expected to perform. In this meaning 'role' is synonymous with 'job' or 'function'. The word has, however, gathered other meanings in the literature of management and organization. For example, we hear or read the expressions 'supervisory role', 'subordinate role', 'staff role', etc. In this sense, role has a meaning which is almost synonymous with 'relationship' (or even, in the case of the first two at least, 'rank'). Then again, we hear of people playing an 'aggressive or dominant role'. Here the emphasis is on the way an individual acts out his role, the particular interpretation that he puts on what he is expected to do and how he is expected to do it. This last meaning is better served by the word 'conduct'.

Each of these meanings of the word role is important to a discussion of organization and a section of this chapter is devoted to each.

Role-function
The role-function is simply the collection of tasks (or 'responsibilities') delegated to an individual, or what the company expects the occupant of a particular position to do. The basic role-function is often reflected in an employee's title, such as recruitment officer, fitter or salesman. The concept of a role-function will differ from one company to another.

We can accept that each role-function should be a compound of several tasks, as long as they are compatible. Occasionally, however, individuals are given or assume more than one role-function. The occupation of multiple roles is rarely a necessity, and should only be permitted when the individual is truly capable of performing the prescribed tasks and when sufficient checks and supports are built into the situation. The owner of a small company who, in addition to acting as overall co-ordinator, assumes the office of Production Manager, may feel that he is the best man available for the job. If this is the case, and if he can devote sufficient time to both roles so that neither suffers from lack of attention, then he may be justified. But more often multiple roles, such as this, are simply the result of malorganization, inability to delegate, or attempted job enlargement, all of which can be contrary to the interests of the business.

To say that a correct role-function is one that expects neither too much nor too little of the role encumbent is almost a truism, yet in practice it is often ignored. At the one extreme 'overloading' executives is commonplace, at the other 'underloading' people is equally widespread. With the former there is the problem of physical and psychological breakdown; the latter leads to lack of job interest and satisfaction. Whatever the role, however vital the output to the company, the dangers of too much or too little are clear.

Rarely is a man asked to perform absolutely incompatible tasks; more often the tasks simply cannot be performed to the right standard in the time allowed. This is one type of role overload. Another is the overload of information. An overload of information occurs when the amount of information provided by established procedures becomes too great for the individual either to assimilate or act upon.

A manager tends to react to either form of overload in several ways, all of which are potentially damaging to the company. He may be forced to delegate tasks to untrained or only partly qualified staff. He may start to form the work in queues, introducing priorities based on his own judgement, or the desire to please, or the pressures exerted from outside; rarely are the priorities the right ones for the company. Again, he may extend his working hours, take work home. Worst of all, he may ignore information or use it incorrectly.

The dangers of 'underload' are possibly just as great; but the connection between the supposed effects and 'underload' itself lacks conclusive proof. On a simple level, Parkinson's Law, that work expands to fill the time allowed, provides a warning. Writers have stated that in most organizations the jobs at the lower levels do not provide opportunities for employees to gain full satisfaction from their

102

work. Man is no better than a machine unless he is allowed some choice, some opportunity to decide how he will behave in a given role.

The final point to be made about role-function concerns the extent to which the function should be defined. It is a question which has received much attention in this book and elsewhere. Here it is intended merely to reiterate and reinforce the statement of the dangers of over-definition.

Previously we have subscribed to the theory that a manager who is allowed greater discretion in the way he achieves his objectives, is a more effective manager. And we have concluded from this that definitions of 'responsibilities' or roles should be concerned mainly with objectives rather than mechanics. This is not enlarging the job, but simply removing the restrictions and allowing the manager to get full satisfaction from the achievement of results which are 'all his own work'.

Even if the theory that greater freedom leads to more effective performance were not true, over-definition would still cause practical difficulties. A manager may find part of his job defined as follows: 'control figures must be prepared by the 5th of each month; they must balance exactly and be 100 per cent accurate in all respects; they must be agreed with the Financial Director'. The requirements are clear and explicit. But what if the Financial Director is absent for six weeks or the figures are £0·1 out of balance on the 5th?

Role overload, underload and over-definition lead to conflict for the role occupant. The specification of roles should be designed to avoid such conflict, but, since people have different needs and abilities, a decision will have to be made in each case whether the fault lies in the specification of a role or the inadequacy (or superiority) of the manager for the role.

Role-relationships
Just as an organization is an open system relying on its environment to accept its output and provide input, so each unit in an organization is an open sub-system relying on interaction with other units for its survival. Carrying the principle even further, we can say that each role can only be performed by interaction with other roles. The operator can only perform his job if his machine is properly maintained, if material is supplied, if he is paid and so has the means of renewing his

103

physical strength, if he gets satisfaction and so has the desire to do the job, etc. Each role has a relationship to other roles, which is vital to its correct functioning.

The main types of relationship which are formally recognized by most companies are three in number: 'direct' or 'line' relationships, 'functional' or 'staff' relationships, and 'lateral' relationships.

Direct relationships are those between a superior and his immediate subordinates. The superior exercises formal authority over his subordinates, and the subordinate in turn is accountable for his performance to his superior. The relationship officially is one of command and compliance. The Production Manager has such a relationship with his foremen; the foremen with their charge-hands; the charge-hands with their operators.

Often the alternative description, 'line', is used to refer only to departments closely connected with the production process. If we must categorize departments in this way, it may be time for some rather more descriptive and meaningful terms – perhaps 'operational' and 'supportive'. Our main concern in this context, however, is with relationships between roles rather than departments.

The superior/subordinate relationship is a two-way relationship, both upwards and downwards. But not only is it different in type for the superior and his subordinate, it is also different in number; to be more explicit, the supervisor may have formal authority over several subordinates, but each subordinate may have only one boss; at least the principle of Unity of Command states that this should be the arrangement. Fayol said quite plainly that 'an employee should receive orders from one superior only'. In this form the principle is unacceptable from a practical point of view. The principle is more acceptable if it is interpreted not as 'unity of order-giving' but 'unity of accountability'. A man should have only one boss in the sense of the person to whom he must ultimately account for his actions. He may, however, receive instructions, requests and pressures from other sources. For example, in a highly decentralized, divisionalized company, recruitment of personnel may be carried out on a divisional basis. Yet wage rates may be the subject of company-wide policy. A recruitment officer receives instructions from the divisional head to recruit more staff; and he must carry out this task or account for his failure to the divisional head. He is also bound by company policy to offer certain wages. He feels pressure

104

from at least two sources, therefore, but he is ultimately accountable to one person.

When specifying a direct relationship, therefore, we may feel it necessary to state the possible sources of orders descending on a particular role. As the minimum, we should identify the primary source and the person to whom the role incumbent is ultimately accountable.

The majority of people who influence operations in a given department have a series of direct relationships linking them to the head of the department. But since every department relies on other departments for its functioning, as well as its own operations, members of these other departments will have some official relationship to members of the original department. Often the members of other departments are called specialists, since their relationship is not one of command on a general front but influence in a limited range of activities. These are known as 'functional' or 'staff' relationships.

Functional or staff relationships take several specific forms, but basically the specialist supplies assistance which in theory can be accepted or rejected. This assistance may take the form of information and advice or may be the performance of a service – there may be a functional relationship between a recruitment officer and the production manager. The recruitment officer engages staff for the production manager, but he is accountable to the personnel manager. Wherever an outsider, not in a direct relationship to a departmental head, influences the operations of a department, a functional relationship (implying assistance and acceptance) should exist.

The specialist can be from a higher or lower organizational level than the manager whose department he serves; he may be a company secretary and legal specialist advising the copy-writing manager on the legality of a particular advertising claim, or a work study engineer timing a job in the production department. In theory, neither the specialist nor the person served can give orders to the other; there is no formal authority implicit in the relationship. But conflict between managers and specialists is commonly caused by the attempt to exercise such authority, where the true nature of the relationship has not been made clear to those involved. The specialist has no formal authority in the departments that he serves. He may, however, exercise 'actual' authority and possess 'personal' (or 'sapiential') authority. The principle remains intact: from the standpoint of formal, theoretical organization,

105

the specialist can only offer assistance and the manager accepts or rejects the assistance.

Lateral relationships are the third group of formal relationships in organization structure. It is unfortunate that many companies do not recognize the need to specify lateral relationships, since they are vital to the achievement of company objectives. To a large extent, they are themselves implicit in the hierarchy of objectives; it may be clear that the achievement of two objectives is a prerequisite and a means to achieving a 'higher', more comprehensive, objective. A lateral relationship, therefore, is usually one between employees on the same organizational level, between for example a production manager and a sales manager. If there is a company objective of increased sales, there must be co-operation between selling and producing functions. Only with higher production can sales increase; so production and selling targets combine to achieve overall marketing objectives. The essence of lateral relationships, therefore, is mutual co-operation on the same organizational level.

A brief comment about the special case of the personal assistant is necessary, since many companies refer to such a role as having 'staff' relationships with other managers.

The existence of personal assistants is usually justified on two grounds. First, they help to relieve an overburdened top manager without diluting his formal authority (in fact, they can increase his Span of Control), and second, the position of personal assistant provides an excellent training. The P.A. is seen as particularly useful in performing a function company-wide which is not handled by divisional personnel; especially where geographical dispersion is a feature, it allows the top executive to be, as it were, in two or more places at once. The more personal assistants a man has, however, the more likely it is that he is using them for jobs which could be delegated to divisional personnel.

A greater difficulty may be in the personality of the assistant. If he is ambitious and forceful, he may try to assume authority which he does not formally possess. If he is weak, he will be ineffective in the role. Officially he has no authority of his own, only by virtue of his connection with the top executive. He must be trained to think and act as his boss would. His activities, like his boss's, must be of a general nature; if he specializes, he is in danger of undermining the authority of heads of specialist departments.

106

The formal relationships between a P.A. and other members of the organization are clear; in fact, he has only one – a direct relationship with the man he assists. Every task he performs is officially the task of his superior. The particular task he is performing at a given time may be accompanied by a particular relationship, direct, functional or lateral, depending on the relationship his superior has with the other employees involved. So, just as the role should be specified, so the assistant (and other employees) should be conscious of the relationship he is taking over temporarily from his superior.

Role-conduct
A role is born when a formal prescription of activities and relationships is laid down. It reaches maturity when it is performed by a human being. However clear the prescription and however good the selection of the role occupant, the resemblance between the formal and the performed role will never be exact. No two people will ever perform a role in the same way. In this respect, the theatre is an analogy. Writers conceive a role; each new actor gives it a different interpretation. It may be that definitions are not sufficiently precise; but this is not a fault, since every individual must be allowed some choice in the way he performs a role, otherwise he is no better than a machine. Everyone expects certain satisfactions from the roles he accepts; he must be allowed to receive these satisfactions while fulfilling the formal requirements of the roles.

People often find difficulty in assuming a new role. A recently promoted manager may not be able to refrain from involvement in details; for a long time he may refuse to delegate. On the other hand, he may make a complete and sudden change, employing the methods and practices which he previously condemned in his own boss, but which he regards now as the right behaviour for himself.

Personality also affects the success of formally prescribed relationships. It has been shown before that an effective direct relationship depends on the acceptance by the subordinate of the supervisor's guidance. This in turn depends on what we may call the supervisor's approach. At one extreme, a manager simply makes a decision and announces it as a rule. He may be less authoritarian and 'sell' his decision to his subordinates. He may present his ideas and invite questions. He may instead present the problem, and ask for suggestions,

107

but still make the decision himself. Finally, he may permit the work group to discuss and decide. (But at this end of the scale can we really call him a 'manager'?) The 'style' of every manager can be placed at a point on this continuum. The effectiveness of a work group will depend to a large extent on the manager being able to choose the right level of authoritarianism and permissiveness to suit his particular group of subordinates.

Difficulties in the functional relationship of specialists to the managers they serve are rarely caused by any formal oversight. As we have shown, there should be no formal authority implied in the relationship, yet often the specialist will have 'actual' authority as a result of his greater technical ability; and, after all, if a man is employed in a specialist role, we expect his decisions to be right within his field, and to be accepted. If he understands and accepts the nature and limitations of his prescribed relationship with other organizational members, the specialist will not be the cause of conflict.

Summary

Every employee of a company is formally required to perform one major role. The nature of this role is usually reflected in the title of the job. He may also be asked to perform secondary roles.

Role overload, underload and over-definition cause conflict and should be avoided.

Formal relationships are direct, functional or lateral. Direct relationships are those between a superior and his immediate subordinates. They are relationships implying command and compliance. Functional relationships are those between specialists and members of the departments which they serve. They are relationships of assistance and acceptance. Lateral relationships are between employees on the same organizational level, who are not connected by direct or functional relationships but whose work must be co-ordinated. The relationship is essentially one of mutual co-operation. A personal assistant has a direct relationship to his superior; in his own right, he has no other formal relationships.

Personality affects the way a role is performed and the success of relationships. Evidence for this includes the difficulties of people who are promoted to new roles, the need for the supervisor to adapt his approach to suit the particular work group, and the conflict between specialists and the managers they serve.

PART C

People

The first half of this book has been concerned in the main with the mechanics of organization structure, which can be likened to a piano. Now we must consider the pianist. The human relations school are right to point out that even the most brilliantly designed structure can have little effect unless the people are both able and willing to make it work. This is the theme of Part C.

Chapter 9 considers human motivation and its relationship to organization. Chapter 10 examines the natural tendency of people to form groups and the 'unnatural' imposition of groups within an organization. This leads in Chapter 11 to the subject of leadership and its relationship to management. Part C finishes with a chapter dealing with recent trends in the dialogue between organization analysts and the behavioural sciences.

Chapter 9

People and their Needs

The behaviour of people is but a poor reflection of their underlying motivation. Every man has an idea, however vague, of what he is or wants to be and a conception, however distorted, of the world in which he lives and works. He sets out to be himself in the world as he sees it. Often people appear to act like sheep but their reasons for acting in a particular way and their aims are different, if only in detail.

Organizations often require their members to act against what they see as their own self-interest. They may, for example, call for increased output at one time with a lull to follow; to a man with a high need for stability or security this represents a conflict of demands. Again, where individuals work at machines in comparative isolation from each other, the man who enjoys closeness and friendship will feel the mental conflict of having to behave in a way which is contrary to his natural tendency. The results of this clash of personal needs and organizational demands are mental conflict for the individual and a form of ineffectiveness for the organization.

The traditional solution to this problem is the offering of incentives; the individual is compensated for the inconvenience by enjoying some reward. In the past the practice has been to offer incentives mainly in the form of money and increased leisure to spend it. It is now widely accepted, however, that for many people purely financial incentives are insufficient to stimulate effort, and that work, far from being a necessary evil, can in itself be a potential medium for great personal satisfaction to a large number of people.

It is also widely accepted that every man has a variety of needs and that these are arranged in a kind of hierarchy. Those at the bottom are comparatively easy to satisfy in modern Western Society, those at the top require more effort, present more challenge and, for all that, bring more satisfaction in attainment.

For people to behave in a way that an organization demands, there must be an integration of the needs of the people and the demands of the organization. The only effective inducement which can be offered by an organization to an individual is one which the individual accepts as being a means of satisfying his needs and so enhancing the idea he has of what he is or wants to be.

What does all this imply? First we need to know a great deal more about the sort of things which motivate people. We have to accept that the variety of individual mixtures of needs is probably infinite. If we do accept this, then we must further agree that the most effective incentives are completely personal and related to the individual. As a formal proposal, however, for all members of an organization this is not practicable. It is most unlikely that an organization can achieve its objectives while formally catering for every need of its individual members. But it should *formally* recognize and appeal to the most important, most strongly felt and most common of the motives of its members, and going one step further, it should train supervisors to recognize and allow *informally* for the individual varieties of motives of their subordinates.

Motives – Classical Theories and Practical Thinking

The difficulties of knowing what makes some people tick are increased by the fact that the individual himself has only an incomplete realization of his motives. To Freud we owe the 'discovery' of unconscious motivation, the idea that the real causes of a person's behaviour may be unknown even to that person. Freud himself stressed the underlying motives of self-preservation and pleasure-seeking. Adler, a one-time associate of Freud, emphasized the power-seeking motive. The young child has a great deal of power to influence the behaviour of others. Some children are allowed to retain this power to the point where it becomes an habitual craving and the adult society causes frustration. Another theory postulates love of self, love of belonging, love of creation and love of service as prime motives.

At a shallower but altogether more practical level we have the following motives:

Survival
Self-esteem
Prestige
Protection of Ego
Security
Pride
Greed
Belonging
Acceptability
Power
Competence
Achievement
Personal Growth

Any list is certain to be incomplete, but every individual is likely to have a number of those above. The mixture and strength of the motives will vary enormously from one person to another.

To be effective, an incentive should be designed and presented in such a way that the person to whom it is offered will see it as a means of satisfying one of his dominant motives. Therefore, a greater understanding of human motives is required both by those who design a scheme and those who administer it. Furthermore, an organization should be designed and administered in such a way that individuals can satisfy many of their needs, and so that personal satisfaction becomes identified with the success of the organization. This is complete integration.

'Motivators' and 'Hygienic Factors'

It is clear that the power of needs to stimulate behaviour will fluctuate. Generally speaking, once a need is satisfied it ceases to stimulate unless some change in the individual or his environment renews the strength of the need. To grasp this concept it is useful to regard a need as an imbalance. Satisfying a need restores balance. For example, take the simple case of thirst: a thirsty man drinks until his thirst is quenched. After a time his physical state changes (the environment will play a part in determining how soon this happens) and he needs once again to restore a balanced state of body liquid. Although this may be an oversimplification it illustrates the point, and allows us to go further. In a

113

hot climate where water is scarce, the desire to quench a thirst will tend to be a strong motivating force. But to us, living in a climate in which water is normally in good supply, the offer of a bucket of water in return for an hour's work would be unlikely to win our assent: and yet we dislike the inconvenience of having our water supply cut off. It is clear that there are some things which we need and yet which do not stimulate us to action; only if they are removed, do we respond.

This was one of the conclusions of a series of studies carried out by a team under the direction of Frederick Herzberg[1] of the Psychological Service of Pittsburgh. The studies consisted of interviews with engineers and accountants to discover the particular incidents which had given them pleasure and displeasure in their recent experience at work. Despite the obvious restrictions of this method of study (such as the reliance on the memory and bias of individuals) the related experiences showed a remarkable degree of uniformity. It was clear that the things which really stimulated effort were opportunities to handle more challenging and demanding assignments, to become more expert and to develop abilities. These were the real 'motivators'. The traditional incentives of job security and working conditions were merely 'hygienic factors'. The latter stimulated no further effort but had to be maintained to avoid damage to efficiency or morale. As Gellerman has said,[2] 'Hygienic factors are prerequisites for effective motivation but are powerless to motivate by themselves. They can only build a floor under morale.'

The incidents described were also classified into short and long term in the satisfaction or dissatisfaction they produced in the individual. Other factors, such as fair treatment and recognition by superiors which are often considered motivators, tended to give only short-term satisfaction. The ultimate in good, long-term motivation appeared to be when men were pushed to the limit of their capabilities and when jobs which demanded ever-increasing effort were given to men who felt their abilities increasing in proportion.

Herzberg may have chosen to study engineers and accountants because of their growing importance in modern business and technology. They are, however, not typical of all levels of workers and one could object that their greater education precludes generalizations on the basis of the data they supplied. Other studies, however, have confirmed the

[1] See F. Herzberg, B. Mausner and B. Snyderman, *The Motivation to Work.*
[2] *Motivation and Productivity*, p. 49.

114

conclusions of Herzberg and his colleagues. One in particular is worthy of extra attention. The motivational studies at Texas Instruments have been reported by M. Scott Myers.[1] This six-year study examined the motivating forces not only of scientists and engineers, but of 'manufacturing supervisors', 'hourly male technicians' and 'hourly female assemblers'. The three main conclusions of the research effort were: (a) the things that motivate employees are 'a challenging job which allows a feeling of achievement, responsibility, growth, advancement, enjoyment of work itself, and earned recognition', (b) the things that dissatisfy employees are 'mostly factors which are peripheral to the job – work rules, lighting, coffee breaks, titles, seniority rights, wages, fringe benefits, and the like', and (c) workers become dissatisfied 'when opportunities for meaningful achievement are eliminated and they become sensitized to their environment and begin to find fault'.

The moral seems to be, in Gellerman's words, 'Today's motivator is tomorrow's hygiene.' The carrot can cease to provide positive stimulation but it cannot be removed. It must be reinforced by appealing to a new level. To see the implications of this, we can reconsider some of the commonly quoted human needs.

What are the Real Motivators?

At the start, we should emphasize again that not only is 'today's motivator tomorrow's hygiene' but, quite conceivably, one man's motivator is another's hygiene. This is clear in the case of the first human motive we shall consider – the survival motive.

Survival: In underdeveloped countries the physiological needs which seek the means of survival are still very powerful motivators. In more developed countries the need for, say, food and shelter, is not a positive stimulation of action; yet lack of the means of obtaining food will certainly cause dissatisfaction. Our attitude towards food tends to be a latent desire for it to continue to be available. If we know we can satisfy a hunger almost at will, food is an object of indifference for most of us. The desire for survival will only motivate us to act if our survival is threatened.

[1] M. Scott Myers, 'Who are your Motivated Workers?' *H.B.R.*, January/February 1964.

Security: The security motive is closely connected to the survival motive in that there is a wish for continuation implicit in both. It is a natural tendency to want to ensure that oneself and one's family are protected against the hazards of the future. Conscious security motives of this type are extremely common and companies have spent a great deal of time and money appealing to them. But once again it is doubtful whether above a certain minimum satisfaction level this conscious desire for security actually motivates. On the contrary, if a company provides too liberally for the satisfaction of security motives it may instil in its employees too great a desire for permanency with the result that all initiative and creativity are regarded as dangerous.

Prestige: This is the motive commonly identified as the desire to keep up with the Joneses or, better still, to be a Jones. The prestige-conscious man likes to know how others regard him; he enjoys comparisons.

The strength of prestige as a motivator is thought to depend on two things: the dissatisfaction an individual may feel with his origins and the belief he has that improvement of status is possible. Those whose origins are far from humble may be 'above' a prestige motive. The memory of 'rags' has proved for others a strong motivation to acquire 'riches'.

Money can certainly buy some of the symbols of prestige; and the more materialistic our society becomes, the more important these symbols are.

Belonging: The need to conform and be accepted by others is a strong natural motivator, but once an individual has been received into a group his need to belong becomes simply another hygienic factor. If his membership is threatened he will be stimulated to act; otherwise the need to belong is dormant.

In the past, the attitude of organizations to their members' motives of 'belonging' have often been unsatisfactory. The tendency has been to try to suppress this motive, to condemn 'informal' groups. However, far from destroying the need to belong, many companies have found that such action has merely strengthened the informal groups and their resolve to indulge in activities which are contrary to the demands of the organization. The point must be made here that, as with other needs which are predominantly hygienic factors, the need to belong can be a strong motivator if the right to belong is threatened. It is the task of a company not to deny the right or ignore the need to belong, but to

116

encourage the formation of groups whose aims and norms are in harmony with the company's demands and practices.

Competence or Power: The desire to gain mastery over one's environment, to make things happen, to create events is potentially a strong motivator since it can never be completely satisfied. It must be emphasized that not everyone has this motive to the same degree.

Achievement: Often the competence and achievement motives are indistinguishable. In industry, the man with a high achievement motive responds to targets, he tries to reach new levels of performance, he enjoys entering new fields. And unless his work calls for ever higher performance and an increasing variety of talents, the achievement-motivated man is likely to be frustrated.

Achievement was the motivating force in the case of Herzberg's engineers and accountants. It is a very personal motive, similar to the desire of an artist to paint.

Money: It is not intended here to add many more to the millions of words which have already been written about the money motive. Usually, though not always, money is a symbol, a means of achieving satisfaction for many deeper needs, or of relieving many less obvious dissatisfactions.

W. F. Whyte[1] directed a number of studies into the pay and motivation of workers. The incidence of possession of 'pure money motives' he put at about one in ten of industrial workers. He found that, in a sense, workers have a more logical attitude to money than they are given credit for. They will refuse to maximize short-term financial advantages at the risk of long-term security.

Organizations must look beneath the cry for more money to see the real motivation. As Herzberg found, money cannot be a motivator but a hygienic factor.

The Hierarchy of Needs

The foregoing analysis of commonly-found motives has indicated that there may be an underlying order in which we seek to satisfy needs,

[1] *Money and Motivation.*

the physiological needs being at one end of the scale and the desire to gain mastery over the environment (an unsatisfiable ideal) at the other end.

A. H. Maslow[1] proposed that human needs can be arranged in a particular order from the lower to the higher. The lowest needs are physiological: hunger, thirst, shelter; these are essential for survival. Next come safety needs: security, health, protection against actual and potential dangers. Belonging or membership needs are next: affection, closeness, identification. Then we have a need for esteem: self-respect, prestige and success. And finally there is the need for 'self-actualization': personal growth, self-fulfilment, the realization of our full potential.

Maslow suggested that we attempt to satisfy our needs in this order. If we satisfy our needs for food, drink and shelter, we can then be stimulated by the need for security. When our existence is secure, we may want to belong – and so on. If at any level we fail to satisfy our needs, that level will continue to occupy our thoughts and we will never progress beyond.

The Impact of Maturity

Another progression, similar and related somewhat to the move from lower to higher needs, is the growth from immaturity to maturity. And the degree of maturity of an individual is another important determinant of his behaviour.

Argyris examined the psychological differences between children and adults and concluded that seven changes normally took place as an individual grew up. First, from a state of almost total passivity as a child he moves to one of great activity as an adult. Secondly, he grows out of total dependence on others and develops independence. Thirdly, from a very limited range of activities (sleeping, eating, crying, etc.) he develops versatility. Fourth, he ceases to find a new interest with every moment and settles down to a fairly well-established range of interests, each of which can give an adult hours of pleasure at a time. Fifth, his time perspective lengthens; he develops memory, and past, present and future alike concern him. Sixth, he grows out of being a subordinate to everyone and becomes an equal or even a superior. Seventh, he develops an ego and will go to some lengths to protect it.

[1] *Motivation and Personality.*

Even within one age group, individuals will vary in the degree of maturity they have reached along each of these seven lines. The man who still retains much of the dependence of childhood, will crave for security. On the other hand, the more mature individual demands responsibility.

The satisfaction that an individual will find working in an organization depends very largely on the fitness of his degree of maturity for the particular role that he is being asked to play. The restrictive type of organization tends to be a frustrating environment for the more mature man. He is stifled by an atmosphere which dictates that he should do as he is told and leave the thinking to others. His desires for achievement, competence, self-esteem find no satisfaction. The result is frustration for the man and waste for the organization. 'It would seem . . . that organizations have acquired a remarkably effective way of insulating themselves against the kind of people who could make them more viable by inducing them to change.'[1]

On the other hand, for a large number of people the typical organizational atmosphere gives a feeling of security, of direction, of something to depend on.

Recognition and Measurement of Motives

It is a comparatively simple matter to list motives; identifying the motives of a labour force of, say, five thousand is a far more difficult problem. The usual practice has been to work on the assumption (which has some foundation) that money represents many motives to many people, and not to be concerned over individual cases. But, without at least informal recognition of individual motives and adaptation of management and other practices to suit individuals, a great deal of money may be wasted on vain attempts to stimulate co-operative, organizational effort.

The first priority is to develop a means of analysing and recognizing motives. A step in this direction was made by Clare W. Graves in a paper published in 1966.[2] In this paper, Graves distinguishes seven types of behaviour pattern which, like Maslow's hierarchy of needs,

[1] Gellerman, *Motivation and Productivity*, p. 76.
[2] *H.B.R.*, September/October, 1966. The description of types goes a little beyond Graves' analysis.

are arranged in a particular order. Using these behaviour patterns we can try to analyse the motives dominant for each type and propose the structures and management principles which may be appropriate.

The 'autistic' type: His existence is like that of a vegetable. He has little or no drive and is unemployable in the normal sense.

The 'animistic' type: He has some awareness of his environment, but little comprehension. His dominant motive is survival, but he is subject to whims and superstitious beliefs.

The 'awakening' type: He is aware of and frightened by conflicting forces in himself and the world, which he only partly understands. His prime motives are security, preservation of the *status quo.* Rigid rules, procedures, etc., give him comfort and support. He will take opportunities as long as there is no risk to his security.

The 'aggressive, power-seeking' type: He challenges tradition and established rules; he prefers to set his own rules. His dominant motive is power; possibly prestige also. The security motive is dormant. He is difficult to handle and increasing the pressure and rigidity of the rules only makes him worse. A case for delegation with over-ride.

The 'socio-centric' type: He seeks a congenial work atmosphere. He is concerned with social rather than personal or material matters. He enjoys group activities; he is a great committee man. His dominant motive is belonging (in the active rather than the security sense). The prestige and security motives are dormant.

The 'aggressive, individualistic' type: He is self-confident, responsible, ends- not means-oriented. He will resent specifications of methods. He responds to participation in target setting. He likes nothing that is imposed. His dominant motive is achievement. This man is the potential top manager and the type against whom Argyris finds the traditional organization insulated.

The 'pacifistic, individualistic' type: He too is ends-oriented and expects to participate in setting his own targets. His dominant motives are
120

achievement and self-esteem, but he is not concerned about esteem from others. He tends to be self-controlled and rather theoretical.

Any categorization of the human race is certain to be an over-simplification. But since it is managers and supervisors, not psychologists, who have to deal with people at a practical level in industry and commerce, some simplification is essential. Plato's philosopher/king was an ideal type; we may suppose that the psychologist/manager is too. Nevertheless, to separate seven main groups of people and to apply a different management practice to each is a great advance on treating people as one amorphous mass. If managers were to follow these lines, the only result could be improvement; and the better managers will be able to distinguish even finer differences.

Other attempts are being made to analyse and categorize types of people and their motives. The next step should be to measure the strength of motives and their effects. Many human characteristics can be measured, at least relatively, at the present time. Over the next decade or so, it is not inconceivable that many more characteristics, including motives and personality, may prove measurable. When we can identify and measure the strength of a person's motives and the impact of incentives, we can design even better structures and incentive schemes.

Summary
Every man has some idea of what he wants to be and of the world in which he lives and works. On the whole his behaviour is guided by a desire to be 'himself' in the world as he sees it. An organizational situation can be a stressful one for an individual if it demands that he should act against what he sees as his own self-interest.

The traditional reaction of the organization, that is the offering of mainly financial incentives, is often inadequate.

The real answer is an integration of the needs of people with the demands of the organization. This is not as difficult as has been thought since many people do have strong motives for achievement, for competence and for prestige, all of which can be satisfied in a work situation; and their satisfaction can greatly benefit a company.

To achieve this integration we must first be able to identify motives.

121

We are certain to find that people differ widely in the mixture and strengths of their motives. We should formally recognize and appeal to the most common and most strongly felt motives, and train managers to identify and appeal informally to each individual's motives.

Not all human needs motivate people to action. True 'motivators' were found in one study to be opportunities to handle more challenging assignments. Traditional incentives, such as job security, etc., were found to be merely hygienic factors; these stimulated no further effort but had to be maintained to prevent losses of efficiency or morale. On examination, it was recognized that all the commonly quoted motives could become merely hygienic factors, except for the competence or power motive, since no individual is likely to gain complete mastery over his environment.

The 'motivator' and 'hygienic factor' theory implies that some needs, once satisfied, will cease to stimulate effort. The same implication is found in the idea that there is a hierarchy of needs, ranging from the lower, physiological needs to the higher needs of self-actualization. It is claimed that we attempt to satisfy our needs in this order.

The degree of maturity of the individual will also influence the way he reacts to organizational situations. Psychologists feel that in many cases organizations are so designed that they try to suppress the very motives whose satisfaction could benefit them most.

The next steps in industrial psychology should be to develop ways of making motives more recognizable and measurable. This will facilitate and improve the design of more effective organizations.

Chapter 10

The Behaviour of Groups

In the previous chapter we touched upon the 'unintended consequences' that may result from a company's neglect of the psychological needs of its employees. For Argyris these unintended consequences are adaptive activities by individuals in response to an environment which gives them little opportunity to have any control over their jobs.

In particular Argyris argues that the traditional organization actually causes these unintended consequences by three mechanisms. First, the organization structure itself, being of a pyramidal type, inhibits the individual's expectation of rapid progress. It also tends to concentrate formal authority in a very few hands; the man at the bottom has little means of determining his own working life; regardless of their individual motives, all are treated alike. Secondly, the power structure is reinforced by 'directive' supervision. The division of labour is: supervisors make decisions, subordinates carry them out. This strengthens unity of direction, but it also increases the apathy and dependence of subordinates. Thirdly, management controls, budgets, capital expenditure restrictions, standard practice instructions, and the like tend to inhibit initiative and ingenuity.

Elsewhere in this book we have considered the pyramidal versus the flat structure, the question of formal authority and the effects of restrictions placed on management. In this chapter we examine the behaviour of groups within organizations, particularly the 'informal' work group. This subject has a direct bearing on our study since the informal group, with aims which may appear to undermine those of the organization as a whole, can be a result of the frustration caused by the mechanistic approach to organization and also, perhaps, the most powerful weapon of the frustrated.

123

The Self-formed Group and its Leader

People have always banded together into groups. There are two sets of reasons for this – material and psychological. On the material plane, there is the need for sheer weight of numbers for reasons of physical work (as in erecting Stonehenge), or for weight of opinion (as in the formation of Trades Unions); and there is the need to specialize to get the task done better, allowing the strong to concentrate on lifting the heavy loads, while the more intelligent do the calculations.

The psychological reasons include the attractions of group security and avoidance of individual responsibility, and there is the satisfaction in the achievement of a shared task beyond the individual's own conceptual or physical abilities.

In such self-forming or informal groups, the emergence of a leader seems inevitable to satisfy the intrinsic needs of the group. A leader is needed as a focal point for concerted action, for without him all would be pulling in different directions. A leader, too, is needed as a representative – a voice and a symbol of what the group is aiming to do, and he is needed as a father-figure to satisfy some of the psychological needs of its members. Certain people in the group will emerge as better at some of these special tasks of leadership than others, and will act as the leaders – possibly different leaders for different situations.

To rely on self-formed groups and emergent leaders is not, however, sufficient for business organizations. Business activity is certainly best organized by groups but these will be formed by the company and their tasks will be specified by the company. Nevertheless within the formal framework of organized groups, the emergence of informal groups based on friendships and common interests is inevitable. And it is important that organizations should be planned with an awareness of both the existence of such groups and the potential dangers and benefits of their existence.

Types of Group

It is a commonplace that no individual in an organization is a member of only one group. Rather he moves from one group to another, and may be in more than one group at any one time. How this can happen is explained by the nature of the various types of group, of which there are basically three in number, the 'command' group, the 'task' group

124

and the 'informal' group. The last of these we have called a single type though in numbers, organization and purposes such groups may be very diverse. The important fact is, however, that most organizations *formally* recognize both command groups and task groups, but not groups based on friendships, common interests, etc., which are called *informal* groups.

The most obvious type of group in any business organization is the command group. Command groups consist of the superior and his subordinates and as such are the building blocks of the organizational hierarchy. The whole organization is composed of interconnecting command groups, with each individual, except at the highest and the lowest level, being both a supervisor in his own command group and a subordinate in that of his superior.

Closely related to the command group is the task group; though the two need not coincide, they often do. Task groups consist of those members of the organization formally assigned to carry out a particular function or task. Each individual may have a definite part to play in the function of the group, but the essential characteristic is that the group itself has an objective and the operations of the group members are necessary for the achievement of that objective.

These two then are established by the organization to meet the needs of the organization. They may not, however, meet the needs of the individuals in the organization. In the majority of cases the individual's need to belong is satisfied by his membership of friendship or common interest groups not formally recognized by the organization. Such groups infiltrate and superimpose themselves on the formal group structures and can have serious, detrimental effects on the functioning of the organization.

The Strength of Informal Groups

Concentrated interest in the causes, existence and effects of groups was catalysed by the studies at the Hawthorne Plant of the Western Electric Co. Elton Mayo's work there dispelled the illusion of the 'rabble hypothesis', and established clearly that the effect of informal groups could cut either way. With the girls in the relay test room, he found norms of mutual co-operation to achieve a high level of performance and productivity. This was thought to be a direct result of the interest that management was taking in the work and the fact that the girls were given a degree of control over the conditions of work, albeit a small degree in the form of prior consultation. The opposite effect was observed in the relay bank wiring room. The prevalent attitudes among the men were anti-management and anti-productivity. Output was restricted; the high-performer was an outcast from the informal group, though still a member of the task group.

Other researches have generally confirmed Mayo's findings. Zaleznik and a team of colleagues from the Harvard Business School concentrated their studies on the sources of strength of the informal group. They found that the common norm of such groups was low production. Among the 'outsiders', however, were both 'rate-busters' and low-producers. The question was posed concerning the motivation of the rate-busters. Were the incentives, offered by management, actually getting through to this minority? If so, how and why? The obvious conclusion was that the rate-busters were motivated by the usual incentives and at the same time were indifferent to the associations in which the majority indulged. Not satisfied with this, Zaleznik continued the research and the more data that were uncovered, the clearer it became that the influence of the group was far stronger than that of management, even on the performance of the rate-busters. 'Acceptance by the group was the key motivator, even for those who didn't belong.'[1] The low-producing 'outsider' was adopting the norm of the group in an effort to attract its attention and gain entry. The rate-buster was seeking revenge for exclusion, by pointing out the contrast between the group's norm of productivity and the level which could be attained in reality.

Another research project into the causes of informal groups was conducted by Schachter of the University of Minnesota. As an experiment he exposed his subjects to an expectation of intense pain. The mere thought of misery he found was sufficient to drive people, who had previously had little association with each other, to seek one another's company. Similar observations led Schachter to conclude that perhaps the need for closeness as an end in itself is not as widespread or as strong as is normally supposed. The usual cause of such associations as the subversive group in industry is not a natural yearning for togetherness but a way of adapting to the frustration of the traditional work situation. 'Everyone else is "beaten" by the system, therefore, it is less of a reflection on each individual to be beaten.'[2]

[1] Gellerman, op. cit., p. 57.   [2] ibid., p. 118.

'What emerges from Schachter's work is a somewhat clearer under-standing of why men sometimes form groups which have the effect of lowering productivity. The group itself is defensive in nature. It is a means of creating an artificial, miniature world in which the things that are lacking in the real workaday world – pride, importance, security – are reproduced on a smaller scale.'[1]

We can draw certain conclusions about the informal group from these researches. First, we must accept that informal groups exist. We cannot ignore them, and it can be dangerous to attempt to suppress them. They are a means of creating an environment in which the individual can find certain of the personal satisfactions which are lacking in the formal work situation. Often the cement which holds the group together is a common grievance or a shared distress. The effect of some management practices is to strengthen the bond.

Informal groups with the norm of subversion are not inevitable in all organizations. Where each individual has the opportunity to satisfy some of his personal motives, the common grievance or the shared distress will not exist. Where individuals know that they have a greater measure of control over their environment, they will not feel at its mercy and wish to seek the safety of numbers. If informal groups exist they need not be anti-management and anti-productivity.

Management practices which show an appreciation of the needs of employees can create an atmosphere in which co-operative effort and performance improvement are the norms of the informal group.

This introduces the subject of superior/subordinate relationships and the important concept of the manager's role as group leader. Earlier in this chapter it was emphasized that the totally self-formed group with its intrinsic needs and emergent leader was not sufficient for business organization. For the extrinsic needs of the company the emergent leader may be unsuitable. Group leaders are, therefore, required from two directions – from the natural needs of the informal group, and the imposed needs of the company.

But what is leadership? What has it to do with management? Can good leadership really improve an organization's chances of success? What are the qualities of a good leader? These questions are fundamen-tal to a study of organization structure, and as such form the subject of the next chapter.

[1] ibid., p. 120.

Summary

Argyris found that the traditional type of enterprise can cause certain 'unintended consequences' by means of three mechanisms: the organization structure, directive supervision, and management controls.

One of these 'unintended consequences' is the growth of 'informal groups'. Many researchers have studied the causes and strengths of informal groups. Their studies show that such groups are widespread and provide the individual with an environment in which he may get satisfactions which are denied in the real work situation and a means of sharing with others a common grief or distress. However, it has been shown that where individuals have adequate control over their jobs either they will not need to enter into associations with each other, or, if they do, the group norms can be ones of co-operative and productive activity.

Chapter 11

Leadership and Management

The Relationship between Leadership and Management

The view that leadership is somehow not part of management has been promoted by some writers. A more productive view starts with the assumption that the leadership element is an essential part of every manager's make-up. If it were possible to define it in this way, it would be helpful as the first step in harnessing, applying and exploiting it. Certainly the work of every manager requires him to possess the leadership element. Since group activity is an essential part of business organizations, and since self-formed groups and emergent leaders will rarely satisfy the company's needs in addition to their own, the man appointed at the head of the organized group must possess the ability to lead as well as the ability to handle the 'statistics', etc. The leadership element is an essential part of successful management, whether it be management of a group of half a dozen people or of several thousands.

At any level the leader has to provide three things – direction, drive and representation. He directs by eliminating uncertainties as to what should be done, and by co-ordinating all effort in the group to pull in one direction. He provides drive by getting the group to want to go in that direction. This involves motivation with all its implications, resolving as far as possible those intrinsic needs of the group, and building the leader's own force of personality to evoke 'followership'.

Representation was described by Urwick when he wrote: 'The first function of a leader is representation – to represent the purposes of the group he leads, both to the outside world and to those collaborating with him.'[1] The leader represents the group to the outside when for example the Head of Quality Control attends a management meeting, or

[1] In Tannenbaum, Weschler and Massarik, *Leadership and Organisation: A Behavioural Science Approach*, McGraw-Hill, 1961.

when the Managing Director goes on a trade mission overseas. The leader represents the outside world to the group when, in each of these cases, he returns to the group, keeps the group task in true total perspective, and keeps them informed so as to maintain the right direction and drive.

We can define leadership as: that part of a manager's activities by which he influences the behaviour of individuals and groups towards a desired result; it depends upon the skills and personality of the manager to meet the intrinsic and extrinsic needs of the group he leads.

There are many leadership definitions serving various purposes. This one is aimed at simplicity and at its inclusion as part of management so that it can be treated as a practical, trainable subject which gets results.

An impressive example of the value of first-class leadership comes not from business but from the less controversial field of cricket. During the years 1946 to 1967, Surrey County Cricket Club were county champions on eight occasions. The five seasons during which Surridge was captain accounted for five of these occasions and he could also be said to share the responsibility for two further championship successes in the two years immediately following his retirement. Surridge himself was an average performer with bat and ball; his specialization was leadership. Of course, he had a good side, but their performance must have owed much to him. In business organizations leadership needs to be sustained for longer periods and perhaps in more complex situations, but should we not make better planned use of such result-getting qualities?

Leadership Traits

What are the qualities of men like Surridge? Can we draw up a list of traits of successful leaders? If so, perhaps we would be able to see what a leader should be, to select and develop leaders.

One can attempt to analyse great leaders and draw up a list of the key qualities which made them successful. In some respects this can be an illuminating exercise, but it has several shortcomings. The lists of traits grow longer and longer, and the analysts preparing them often disagree on the important ones. One book quotes seventy-nine traits

130

taken from a number of different lists.[1] But worst of all, perhaps, even when kept short and to one man's opinion, such lists can amount to a specification of unattainable perfection.

The real harm is done when a preoccupation with traits precludes other aspects of leadership, notably that which relates to the situation. The type of leader and style of leadership required for one situation is quite different for another, even for the same group. A situation can change from calm to crisis, from co-operation to militancy, from simplicity to complexity, and a different kind of leadership is required for each.

Research in other fields has confirmed this phenomenon about groups and their leaders. Maslow reports that among the Blackfoot Indians there are no general leaders with general powers, but one for war, one for arranging Sun Dances, one for raising stock, and so on.[2]

On the basis that any one general leader needs to have a whole range of styles to suit different situations, any list of desirable traits drawn from one situation alone must be of limited use. What is true of the wartime leader, geared to situations of emergency, is not applicable to an industrial leader geared to the maintenance of calm. As one American writer puts it: 'The leader is not a disembodied entity endowed with unique characteristics. He is the leader only in terms of his functional relationship to the group.'[3] It is only when this is accepted that discussion of personality traits has any useful meaning.

Remembering this, there are some characteristics of particular importance which can be listed; these are: Integrity, Intelligence and Knowledge, Human Sympathy, Tough-mindedness, Self-awareness.

Integrity. Almost every authority quotes this characteristic, from the theorists to the pragmatists like Lord Montgomery who believes the acid test to be: 'Would I go into the jungle with that man?'[4]

Intelligence and Knowledge. The leader must have knowledge of his subject, or one particular part of his subject, in which he can with

[1] Charles Bird, *Social Psychology*, Appleton-Century, 1940.
[2] *Eupsychian Management*, Richard D. Irwin Inc., 1965.
[3] C. G. Browne and Thomas S. Cohn, *The Study of Leadership*, Interstate Printing and Publishing, 1958.
[4] *The Path to Leadership*, Collins, 1961.

131

judgement be right most of the time. There can be no lasting leadership where a man does not know what he is talking about. This knowledge must be backed by the intelligence to know how and when best to apply the knowledge in any situation.

Human Sympathy. What is required is a balanced view between the extremes represented by the ordinates of Blake's Managerial Grid – concern for people and concern for results.[1] A leader is doomed if he regards people as either a nuisance, or as his only interest.

Tough-mindedness. This is the mark of the mature man who can be single-minded and do what is required by the situation in spite of side-effects. This is the ultimate test – to be able to overcome opposition, to withstand the temptations of short-term compromises, to overcome personal disappointments.

Self-awareness and the impulse to lead. Much has been written about the psychology, the drives and motives of the leader. One school of thought claims that the best leaders are supremely unconscious of their role, but a bigger school believes them to be very aware of themselves, their abilities, and their aims in life. Zaleznik for example defines the major psychological factor in the leader as 'a heightened sense of self'.[2] He describes this as both a resource and a hazard – a resource since from it grows the ability to be tough-minded and to be in self-control, and a hazard since it can push that drive to the neurotic area where he *must* lead rather than *wishes* to lead. The border-line is narrow.

This self-awareness is evident from what Churchill wrote after the war: 'In my long political experience I had held most of the great offices of state, but I readily admit that the post that had now fallen to me was the one I like best. Power for the sake of lording it over fellow creatures or adding to personal pomp is rightly judged as base. But power in a national crisis, when a man believes he knows what orders should be given, is a blessing.'[3] This is the healthy selfishness of the leader from which others benefit.

[1] R. Blake and J. Mouton, *Grid Organization Development*, Gulf Publishing, 1968.

[2] 'Human Dilemmas of Leadership', *Harvard Business Review*, November/December, 1967.

[3] E. E. Jennings, *The Executive*, Harper and Row, 1962.

132

Training in Leadership

It is the situational definition of what the leader does, rather than what he is, which provides the more realistic approach to specific training – in spite of disbelief that leadership can be trained. Disbelief is based on the two maxims that leadership is an art, not a science, and that leaders are born not made. The false assumption is that the two are exclusive alternatives, that we must choose art or science, to be born or made. Supremacy in any art is based on mastery of technique, whether it be painting, acting, piano-playing or leadership. The art lies in the creative skill with which the techniques are applied. Similarly, to be born with the attributes for a particular role does not mean that training cannot help to develop them, nor does the existence of training eliminate the advantage of being born with natural abilities

What can be done practically about developing leadership? Two things are vital – building the right climate and organizing specific training. The first is necessary to ensure the development of a climate which not only allows leadership to grow but positively encourages it.

The second aspect to be covered is the organization of specific training sessions, self-development programmes, and planned experience through job rotation and promotion. These are all regular features of any management development scheme and the only point which needs emphasis here is the subject matter of training sessions. In subject matter, such a course has much in common with general management training, but certain items, which are sometimes not included, require special treatment. These are:

1. Individual and group behaviour – including some psychology, sociology and other behavioural sciences; subjects which receive scant attention in some management courses.
2. Communication – explaining the links between language, understanding, thinking and behaviour. Communications provide the very means of leadership: if there are no words, nothing happens.
3 Influencing people – showing the differences between motivation, persuasion, coercion and manipulation, and the uses and abuses of these actions.
4. Use of authority – explaining the types of authority available to the manager (those derived from structure, knowledge and personality) and their links with his responsibilities.

133

5. Styles of leadership – describing the degrees of autocracy, permissiveness, and participation and their effects.
6. Self-awareness – the individual's own abilities, natural styles, strengths, weaknesses, and personal impacts, and their maintenance of perspective and balance.

All these subjects can be taught with real effect and some remarkable results have been achieved, particularly in revealing to a man his impact on others. Above all, the emphasis is on internal realization. Zaleznik says, 'Training oneself to act and react in the ways just discussed may sound like a formidable task. Formidable though it is, the basic necessity is to overcome the sense of inertia to which we are all susceptible from time to time.' He describes the sense of inertia as when 'life and events appear to occur apart from one's own intentions', and goes on, 'As soon as an executive is able to assume responsibility for his own development and in the course of doing so overcomes the sense of inertia, he is on the road to experiencing leadership as an adventure in learning.'[1]

Leadership in Practice
In the course of this chapter we have made four main propositions:

1. that leadership is a regular part of every manager's job;
2. that the leadership of a group can have a marked effect on its results;
3. that leadership can be trained and
4. that leadership arises from a combination of factors and is not simply the personality of a particular man.

It is an expansion of this fourth proposition which introduces the final part of this chapter which is concerned with leadership styles in practice.

There are four main variables which define the style of leadership and type of leader required: the situation within the group, the situation in which the group exists, the people in the group, and the personality of the leader. Of these the situational factors have a major effect, and any analysis of leadership must start from these.

[1] *Human Dilemmas of Leadership*, Harper and Row, 1966.

A differentiation has been made between the situation within the group and that in which the group exists because they can be independent of each other. There may be a state of crisis in a group which is part of a smooth-running organization, and each influences the leader's task differently.

The third factor, the group's people, may vary in intelligence, education, status, interests and motives; they may be loyal, long-serving, right-minded citizens, or aggrieved, casual, wrong-minded troublemakers. Most probably they are a mixture of them all, but as far as groups can be identified, a quite different style of leader is obviously needed for each type of group.

The leader's own personality, the fourth variable, is unlikely to be as variable or flexible; he is almost certain to be better equipped by nature for one type of situation than for the whole range. So we find the position of a wide range of situations and people to be led, often in a state of flux. Against this we must match leaders usually with a much narrower range of natural abilities. Here is an area of work for industrial sociologists – to define jobs in terms of behaviour as well as responsibilities.

Assuming that the leader interprets all four variables for a particular situation, there is one more variable – his choice of an appropriate style of leadership. The range of styles may be represented by the three terms Autocratic, Democratic and Laissez-faire. These are three points on a scale of more or less dictatorship, more or less participation. Most leaders tend to use all of these styles to some extent over a period of time, but each individual has a natural bent towards or has built up a firm preference for one of them. Each can be more successful in certain situations and it is possible to give some general guidance. A more autocratic or dictatorial approach is appropriate where the degree of crisis in the group and its feelings of uncertainty are high; where the organization in which the group works has itself a highly autocratic climate; and where the personality of the leader is oriented towards ends and is inclined to be egotistical. A style towards the more democratic or participative end is indicated when the past success of the group is high; where the company itself is efficient and stable; where the people in the group are intelligent, feel secure, are satisfied with their lot; and where the leader himself feels secure.

These are illustrations of principle rather than detail; as indicators

135

they are more likely to be right than wrong, but they cannot be more precise because leaders are neither completely aware of the needs of their situations, nor are they so in control of their own abilities that they can choose and apply the appropriate style as from some first-aid medical kit. Training will stretch the leader's awareness of some of his situations and the control of his abilities to meet them, but try as he may he will never be completely flexible – and so much the better since the thought that a leader might attempt to be all things to all men is itself suspect. There is the risk that he will try to assume cloaks of personality which are not his and so sacrifice that essential integrity. There is the worry, too, that a leader who behaves in one way today and in an entirely different way tomorrow is a difficult man to work for. Again the answer lies in the fuller understanding by the leader of himself and his role.

At its simplest, the style of leadership comes down to one basic question: how much dictatorship and how much participation? These extremes are represented by McGregor's theories X and Y,[1] and are implicit in Blake's *Managerial Grid*[2] and Likert's 'employee-centred and production-centred supervision'.

Most people who have met the problem in practice oscillate between the two over a number of years. They may start with the assumption that, as bosses, they give the orders. They do so and succeed in getting short-term results, but find that resentment is built up, that all-out effort by the group is held back, and that long-term results suffer. They may then aim at full participation, only to find that it is pointless trying to please everyone, and that the process takes too long to use consistently, particularly at times of crisis.

One of the most revealing statements that McGregor made about this is worth quoting, particularly since he is widely regarded as a protagonist of the participative school. In this statement he is reflecting on several years of consultancy work in a number of organizations. 'I believed', he said, 'that a leader could operate successfully as a kind of adviser to his organization. I thought I could avoid being a "boss". Unconsciously, I suspect, I hoped to duck the unpleasant necessity of making difficult decisions, of taking responsibility for one course of action among many uncertain alternatives, of making mistakes and taking the consequences. I thought that I could operate so that everyone

[1] See Chapter 4. [2] Op. cit.

would like me – that "good human relations" would eliminate all discord and disappointment. I could not have been more wrong.'[1]

That quotation echoes what many have found for themselves. There are reasons for using participative methods but none of them is the avoidance of the responsibilities of being a boss.

It is the Democratic style of leadership which is the most successful general-purpose pattern. The Democratic leader is characterized by the following:

- he represents both the group and the outside world whereas the Autocrat represents the company view, and the Laissez-faire leader is simply one of the group.

- he explains the reasons behind his orders, and keeps his group informed of future plans.

- he consults them on problems, but does not aim at consensus decisions: their views are taken but the final decision must be his.

If the Democratic pattern is the best, what of the others? Laissez-faire can be seen as a special case where there is need for a group representative but little more: the group makes it own decisions. A small creative or development group might work to this style of leadership.

The Autocratic style, in its worst forms, can cause resentment, absenteeism, and resignations, but it must be considered for several reasons: first because there may be too little time for full participation, particularly at times of crisis – and it has been proved that such leadership gets the highest productivity in the short term; second, because the situation may not permit normal consultation – there may be, for example, other confidential factors involved; third, because the leader not only has authority of position but also of knowledge – he is the expert and will gain nothing from consulting his group; fourth, because with many types of group the drive and direction obtained from such leadership will more than compensate for loss of participation.

This last is a great advantage over other forms of leadership – the sheer impetus of being carried along by one man. How far a man can use it depends on his own leadership skill – the trust he has built up in his group, the example he has set, his maturity in controlling himself

[1] 'On Leadership', *Antioch Notes*, May, 1964.

and going it alone, and the projection of his personality to carry him through. This can be the key difference between good and mediocre leaders – the ability to be tough when the occasion demands it; the ability to change occasionally from the Democratic to the Autocratic style; the ability to provide drive and thrust.

Summary
Leadership is defined as that part of a manager's activities by which he influences the behaviour of individuals and groups towards a desired result; it depends upon the skills and personality of the manager to meet the intrinsic and extrinsic needs of the group he leads. As such, leadership can be trained and good leadership brings results. The basic qualities of a good leader are integrity, intelligence and knowledge, human sympathy, tough-mindedness and self-awareness.

Four variables define the style of leadership required in practice: the situation within the group, the situation in which the group exists, the people in the group and the personality of the leader. The leader's success, therefore, depends on his identification of these factors and a correct choice of leadership style. The choice is not, however, completely free since each individual has a natural bent towards a particular style. The available styles can be represented as on a scale from Autocratic, through Democratic to Laissez-faire. The Democratic style appears to be the most suitable pattern for general purposes, but the ability to switch occasionally, when necessary, to the Autocratic is the skill which separates many good leaders from mediocre leaders.

Chapter 12

People, Organizations, and Change

The uniqueness of each individual member of an organization and the presence of a number of needs peculiar to himself which each individual seeks to satisfy are important aspects of organization. Various behavioural scientists, such as Abraham Maslow, Douglas McGregor, Chris Argyris, Frederick Herzberg, have paid considerable attention to these aspects. Basically this is the approach of the individual psychologist, where the individual worker, or member of the organization, is the basic unit for consideration and the starting point for theories on managing the human relations aspects of an enterprise.

On the other hand the social psychologist stresses the importance of group membership for an individual. The group can be formal or informal but is small and is usually referred to as a 'primary' group, i.e. one in which its members have frequent and regular 'face to face' contact. One of its important aspects is that in several ways a group of this kind has an existence and entity over and above those of its individual members. Thus a team working on, for instance, production study or operational research will still continue to exist even though the people in it change from time to time. This is an example of the more formal small group, but even in informal work groups there are ideas and norms held in common which are pertinent to the group's activities although they may differ in some degree from the ideas of each member. And a group decision may be a working compromise from the decisions of the members, but it is nevertheless a valid decision which to some degree will affect the activities of each individual in the group.

Considerable attention has been paid in recent years to this second entity, the small working group in organizations. Mention has already been made of the classic work carried out by Elton Mayo and his colleagues, and further developments have been made by Rensis Likert, Abraham Zaleznik, and others.

There is a third aspect of people in organizations and this derives from the existence of large organizations themselves. These organizations can be broken down into small groups, both formal and informal, and even to individuals. And yet they have in a sense an existence over and above their component parts, just as primary groups have. And we acknowledge this when we talk of 'company standards' or 'company objectives'. So our individual worker, studied by the individual psychologists, belongs to one or more small groups, studied by the social psychologists, which in turn form a total organization. Although the study of the latter is a comparatively new field in behavioural science, it seems that the sociologist and the anthropologist are the men to contribute most to our understanding.

There are, then, three basic units to consider from the point of view of human behaviour in organizations. First, there is the organization itself, then there is the small work group, and finally the individual. Only by understanding that these three elements exist, and are related, can we really get to grips with the human problems of organizations.

The Characteristics of Human Systems

A number of behavioural scientists who have examined any or all of the three human systems we have chosen – the organization, the work group, the individual – have taken some characteristics from other systems, and particularly biological systems, and drawn parallels in order to clarify some of the elements they have discovered in human behaviour.[1] Two of these characteristics are particularly relevant.

The first of these is the tendency for all human behavioural systems to achieve and maintain a steady state. This is the phenomenon known in biology as homeostasis, and it is observed that when some kind of disequilibrium is caused because, for instance, external forces prevent parts of the system functioning, then the rest of the system reacts to bring it back to its original state. This can be seen in industry when you consider what happens in an organization when there is a sudden drop

[1] For examples, see G. W. Dalton, 'Criteria for Planning Organisational Change' in *Organisational Behaviour and Administration*, Richard D. Irwin Inc., 1965.

in demand for its goods or services, or when a steady supply of raw material or component parts suddenly dries up. In a healthy organization every effort is made to find new customers or new sources of supply so that the former balance is achieved. This does not mean, however, that such a state of equilibrium is a static condition.

The other important characteristic of human systems is their capacity for growth and development, again in common with biological systems. This capacity is more highly developed where human beings are concerned because of their ability to learn. They are constantly receiving 'feedback' about their effect on the environment and on the basis of this they change their behaviour accordingly. Thus the 'equilibrium' state of an organization can be one of steady growth and there is nothing contradictory between homeostasis and a steady company growth rate of x per cent per annum.

The Organization

What requirements must a business organization fulfil to be a fully functioning system?

Dalton[1] suggests six essential elements. First of all there must be the production of goods or services. Secondly, there must be a sales effort to ensure that those goods and services reach those for whom they are designed and to regenerate demand when necessary. Thirdly, there must be a design and development effort to make sure that the products meet consumer demands, and adapt to changes in those demands. In order to bind these first three elements together a fourth element is needed and this is a system of administration and control which relies on effective communication and decision-making.

The final two elements – a system of rewards and punishments, and a company philosophy – are important because of their effect on the individuals within the organization. The rewards, e.g. status, money, etc., must ideally be highly valued by the members of the organization so that they can be used in a way which will encourage activities for the continued health and growth of the company, but will discourage activities which hamper attainment of the company's objectives.

A company philosophy is necessary to generate appropriate attitudes in the individual members and reinforce the motivation given by other

[1] Dalton, op. cit.

141

means, e.g. the rewards and punishments. The ultimate aim is to develop a philosophy which will generate in all members of the organization a loyalty to the purposes of that organization.

If any of these six elements are completely absent, then the system will have difficulty in maintaining itself.

As well as maintenance there is the characteristic of growth, and this can apply to a complete organization just as it can to any other system. Growth is seen not simply in terms of increasing size but also in terms of increasing ability to cope with the circumstances of its environment, e.g. markets, suppliers, etc. Where this potential of growth is not realized in an organization, one can begin to see it becoming inflexible and deteriorating unless changes are made in order to revitalize it. An example of this would be a one-product company whose product declines from market leader to respected 'has-been' as the pattern of demand changes. The decline is not just in the product, it is reflected in the organization.

In order to achieve this growth there seem to be three basic requirements. There must be a feedback system from the environment so that the organization has information as to how its activities relate to the needs of the market. Secondly, if changes are needed, there must be a willingness to change within the organization. Burns and Stalker[1] have given an example of a company which failed to use the advantages of new technology because their old system was not flexible enough to receive it. Finally there must be developed within the organization attitudes receptive to ideas which may conflict with existing policy and philosophy, and be capable of integrating them where it is appropriate.[2]

The Primary Group
As we have seen from an earlier chapter the primary group, both formal and informal, for work or social purposes, represents a very strong element when considering the individual in industrial society. And just as organizations have their own maintenance and growth elements, so do small groups. And in a total organization the presence of small groups can act positively or negatively.

[1] T. Burns and G. M. Stalker, *The Management of Innovation*, Tavistock, 1961.
[2] M. P. Follett, *Dynamic Administration*. Pitman, 1941.

There is sufficient evidence to show that these groups will form spontaneously and can often maintain themselves regardless of the attitude shown towards them by the organization as a whole. Ideally, although this seems rare in industry, an organization should provide the conditions under which these groups can function effectively. The members need a set of activities in which they can join together and participate. If these activities are in line with the objectives of the organization then that organization is likely to be much more effective than one where the reverse is true.

But, in fact, the latter case is the more common situation in business and industry. Much of organizational planning in the past has emphasized the individual rather than the group, and Elton Mayo and his associates discovered that when individuals are successfully isolated there is often high employee dissatisfaction and high labour turnover.[1]

Groups, however, will form in the work situation, even if they only organize social activities or, worse, stimulate activities which run counter to the objectives of the organization. The potential of such groups is often unrealized and many in industry approach what Zaleznik and others have described as 'frozen' groups.[2] The characteristics of these groups have been described as follows:

1. They have few, if any, ways of relating themselves in a positive way to the organizational setting in which they exist. Their aim is to maintain themselves in an environment which seems indifferent, and possibly hostile, to them.
2. The leaders and members of the group have little opportunity to exercise their influence, leadership, and responsibilities other than within the group itself.
3. Even within the group there is a strong tendency to 'sameness' – same activities, same conversational topics, same complaints. There is a lack of growth.
4. There is little opportunity for individual development within the group because of the limitations of the values and aspirations of the group.

[1] E. Mayo, *The Human Problems of an Industrial Civilisation*, Bailey Bros. and Swinfen, 1933.
[2] A. Zaleznik et al., *The Motivation, Productivity and Satisfaction of Workers*, Boston; Harvard Business School, 1958.

Such groups seek to maintain themselves in a defensive, self-centred way and their growth element is almost non-existent. If their attitudes can be 'unfrozen' and their growth stimulated they can be a productive force.

The Individual

We have already seen that an individual belongs to an organization in order to satisfy a number of complex personal needs. These needs have been grouped into five levels on a hierarchy by Maslow – physiological, security, social, esteem, and self-actualization needs. Where these are frustrated in an organization there tends to be unrest, militant unionism, or high labour turnover and absenteeism.

If we now look at this hierarchy of needs in terms of our two concepts of maintenance and growth we can see that as we move up the hierarchy from physiological to self-actualization needs we cover both the maintenance and growth elements. The physiological, security, and to some extent the social needs are all contributory to the effective maintenance of an individual. Some of the social needs, and certainly the esteem and self-actualization needs, are factors in the growth of an individual.

Ideally, therefore, if an organization is to be fully functional at the level of human individuals its aim must be to provide an environment in which individuals can satisfy their full range of needs. In Western industrial society today, and under conditions of full employment, the 'maintenance' element is catered for by most organizations. Attention is now being focused on the 'growth' element and programmes of management development and systems of 'management by objectives' are being designed with this is mind. There seem to be three main elements necessary to facilitate individual growth. Firstly, there must be the opportunity to take self-determined action and responsibility for it, and this must be encouraged. Secondly, the organization around the individual must be sufficiently tolerant so that self-determined action is not seen to be dangerous and mistakes are constructively handled. And finally, each individual must be able to get a clear appraisal and 'feedback' of the consequences of his action.

Leadership

Having considered in some detail the three human systems contained in an organization, we will now return to the subject of leadership in order to see how this approach to an organization gives us further insight into the problems of directing it.

In the last chapter we defined leadership as 'that part of a manager's activities by which he influences the behaviour of individuals and groups towards a desired result' and then went on to examine leadership traits and leadership styles. This was to get at the qualities needed in the human being who is required to play the part of a leader, and the personal attitudes which determine the way he acts.

Let us now turn to the job itself, i.e. the task of leadership as distinct from the person who performs it.

The leader of an organization is handling a number of different entities – the organization itself, a number of formal and informal groups within it, and an even larger number of individuals. Each of these has a number of needs to be satisfied or objectives to be reached. Dominant among these are the objectives of the organization itself, because this is why the organization exists.

The healthiest organization with the greatest potential for growth and the greatest success in human terms will be the organization which can integrate its own objectives with the needs of the people and groups in it. One of the greatest sources of power in the business world is the 'entrepreneur' and much of the psychological strength of the entrepreneur lies in the fact that the satisfaction of his individual needs (e.g. for power, for security, etc.) and the objectives of the organization (*his* organization created in order to satisfy *his* needs) are very closely linked indeed. If he is shrewd enough or fortunate enough in the early days to collect around him a small group of people whose needs are almost identical with his own, or whose needs are satisfied by being willing subordinates, then the organization has tremendous potential for success and growth. As it gets larger, however, the problem of integrating the increasing complexity of needs and objectives becomes substantial and attitudes and styles of leadership become more important.

In a recent book on leadership[1] John Adair, who has studied the subject in military terms in considerable depth, defines the nature of leadership in a similar way. He describes the three elements which

[1] John Adair, *Training for Leadership*, Macdonald, 1968.

145

need integration as the Task, the Team Maintenance, and the Individual Needs in any situation. He describes them pictorially as three partially overlapping circles:

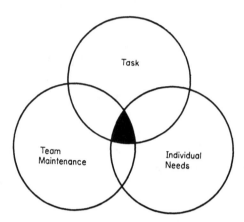

This diagram demonstrates the interrelation of the three elements, with the shaded section representing the ideal situation (hardly ever attained in practice) where complete integration is achieved. If 'Task' is equated to organizational objectives and their attainment, and 'Team Maintenance' to the satisfaction of the needs of particular groups, then Adair's analysis of the nature of leadership in military situations becomes part of the wider analysis reached by behavioural scientists, and military organization can be seen as a specific example of the human systems approach to organizations in general.

The Problems of Change
One of the greatest challenges which faces any twentieth-century organization and its leadership is that of change. In the industrial situation changes in markets and changes in technology, to mention only two areas, exert powerful pressures from outside on organizations which have, if they are to continue to grow, to adapt themselves to such changes. And, internally, the general needs of the individuals within an organization may also change. We have already noted that there is a tendency in Western industrial society to shift from satisfying those individual needs geared to 'maintenance' to those geared to 'growth'. The most obvious example of this is the growing development from
146

'management by incentive' (money for maintenance) to 'management by objectives' (task fulfilment for growth).

Recently the behavioural scientists here began to study the ways in which behaviour in organizations, and leadership styles, vary according to the technology used. Joan Woodward,[1] for instance, has made comparisons between organizations using unit or small batch production, large batch or mass production, and continuous flow-process production methods.

Unit or small batch production usually involves a high degree of craftsman's skills. Quality is more important than quantity, and supervisors tend to share the craft skills with their subordinates, exercising fairly loose overall supervision.

Mass production, however, uses larger working groups and lower levels of skill. Quantity overrides quality, and the task of the supervisor is more in the nature of planning and controlling than exercising craft skills. He also has to be more skilled in man management, as the production method tends to act against the formation of work groups and the satisfaction of social needs within individuals.

With flow-process production methods the operator tends to operate a series of controls. Not a skilled job as such, yet it demands a considerable degree of knowledge of the process and the exercise of judgement, as stoppages are costly. Operators tend to work more independently and require far less supervision than in unit or mass production.

Another study of the impact of technological change, this time on management decision-making, has been made by H. A. Simon.[2] He first of all describes how management problems vary according to how precisely they are structured, how much information one has about them, and how precisely they can be solved. There are, for instance, decisions he describes as 'highly programmed', e.g. the pricing of standard products. On the other hand, 'unprogrammed' decisions are of the one-off type, to enter a new market or develop a new product, etc. In between there are a number of variations, all of them having routine and non-routine elements. But changes in technology (for instance the use of computers and operational research) are valuable

[1] Joan Woodward, *Industrial Organisation: Theory and Practice*, Oxford University Press, 1965.
[2] H. A. Simon, *Administrative Behaviour: a study of decision making*, Collier-Macmillan, 1965.

147

aids in decision-making of the 'highly programmed' type. This does not just mean that managers are spending more time on other decisions, but that they have more time available as much of their routine work is cut down. The problem then is to cope with this change in time availability and make the most productive use of it. A particular case has been described[1] in which an executive spent his available time in (a) conceiving and introducing changes in the system, (b) personnel matters, (c) local community relationships, and (d) improving inter-departmental effectiveness. Not all managers, however, would use their time to such good effect.

These examples of how change can affect organizations and the people within them give some idea of problems that are likely to increase in the future. Where these problems have already been realized organizations have taken steps to prepare themselves and tackle them.

The first approach is through what is now coming to be called the 'change agent'. This is an individual, either a full-time employee or a part-time consultant, whose sole purpose is to advise senior executives on necessary changes, e.g. of organization, departmental structures, systems, etc., and then devise training and other programmes in order that these changes can be installed and operated most effectively. The changes may be inter-personal, inter-departmental, or involving the whole organization. In each case the approach is through the people concerned on the valid assumption that, if the managers and staff accept the change, then that change will be put into operation. The 'change agent' takes as his pattern the formula 'unfreeze present system – install changes – refreeze and maintain new system' and much attention is given to the first step by using T-groups, Managerial Grid Seminars, etc., to generate an analytical and insightful approach in the people concerned so that they question present attitudes and are more receptive to the formation of new ones. The approach makes use of attitudes and feelings as well as of reason.

The possible effects of change have also made themselves felt in the approach to management training concerned with leadership or management style. Many managerial style theorists (such as Blake, Lippitt, etc.) have a tendency to think in terms of an ideal managerial style which is relevant at all times and in all circumstances. One can

[1] In an article by M. Anshen in *Automation and Technological Change*, ed. J. T. Dunlop, Prentice Hall Inc., 1965.

appreciate the theory but find that it does not always work in practice. As we have already seen, different styles of supervision are required for different types of production methods. For a manager who has to change from using one method to using another, the problem is one of changing his own attitude and style of management. From this realization has come the idea of a managerial style continuum ranging from 'highly autocratic' at one end to 'highly democratic' at the other. The main exponents of this idea are Tannenbaum and Schmidt[1] and Reddin.[2] In training managers to use the theories their approach is to try and install a 'flexibility of style' so that a manager can vary his approach according to his analysis of the needs of the situation at any time – and this includes the needs of the people as well as of the organization.

And here we perhaps have a clue to the necessary approach to this whole problem of change. Changes are bound to happen, and will appear more quickly as time goes on. They will all have an effect not only on organizations themselves but more specifically on the people within them. In order to prepare these people to tackle these problems we need to instil in them not only a readiness *for* change but a readiness *to* change, i.e. a flexibility of style and method.

Summary

In this chapter we have analysed three human systems – the organization, the primary group, and the individual – which are seen by behavioural scientists as the elements to be considered when examining the human aspects of organizations.

We have examined each in turn in the light of the two main elements present in all systems if they are to survive – these are 'maintenance' and 'growth'. In order to satisfy these two conditions each system has a number of needs to be satisfied and a number of objectives to be reached. The successful leader of an organization, therefore, is one who can most nearly satisfy the needs of the organization and the groups and people within it at one and the same time.

[1] R. Tannenbaum and W. H. Schmidt, 'How to choose a Leadership Pattern', *Harvard Business Review*, March/April, 1958.
[2] W. J. Reddin, 'The Tri-Dimensional Grid', *Training Directors' Journal*, July, 1964.

Finally we considered the problems of change in an organization. In a world of rapidly increasing technology and fundamental social changes the successful organization will be the one that can adapt itself most readily to the changes in the external environment which affect it and its operations. To achieve this the people within that organization must be flexible in their methods and style – they must be willing to change.

PART D

Practice

It is often difficult in the field of human behaviour to envisage how theories may be applied with success in practical situations. Part D is aimed at displaying the practical side of Organization Study.

Chapter 13 considers the processes of investigation, analysis and diagnosis which necessarily precede structural changes. Chapter 14 discusses and illustrates the uses and abuses of organization charts. Chapter 15 provides some guidelines for the design of structures. In Chapter 16 a number of examples are discussed from the writers' experiences of organizational work; this serves to illustrate both the theories of Parts B and C and the practical approach of Chapters 13, 14 and 15. Chapter 17 draws together many of the thoughts expressed in the earlier parts of the book into a set of organizational dicta. Finally in Chapter 18 we look to the future both of organization research and organizations themselves.

Chapter 13

Diagnosing Structural Faults

Some writers have treated the study of organization as a problem of adapting to growth. Starting with the one-man enterprise, they have outlined the changes that need to be made as the size and scope of the company's operations increase.

It is true that growth itself may cause a company to re-examine its structure, but as a reason for embarking on a reorganization it is no more common than certain other factors. Equally common are the changes introduced following the departure of key personnel from a company, or even the arrival of new blood. Today organizational changes as a result of mergers and take-overs are frequent occurrences. More simply, a change may result from a desire to imitate the structure of a successful competitor, or in response to economic pressures of one kind or another.

The Diagnostician

At an early stage in a company's thinking about reorganization, top management must decide who will be assigned to the task of co-ordinating and supervising the process. Even if he is given a great deal of clerical and analytical assistance, the man who is chosen must possess a number of exceptional qualities. He should be very experienced; and this experience should be broad, rather than deep in one or two specialist fields. He should be a capable negotiator, skilled in human relations; he will need to be accepted and able to convince people at all organizational levels. He should be thrusting and penetrative, yet pleasant.

Companies have adopted a variety of approaches for solving this particular problem of reorganization. In smaller enterprises, one of the executives may be assigned to the task on a part-time basis. Although

153

this has the merit of being less costly than other solutions, it has inherent drawbacks. The company with a small management team is least able to afford to allow one of its top men (and a top man it must be) to neglect his own job. In any case, there is always the human difficulty that pride in his own job and department may lead him to give more prominence to that job or department in the reorganized structure.

Larger companies often have full-time organization planners or developers. Where these are successful, their background and personality approximate to those described above. Some chief executives delegate the task of organization planning to a management committee consisting of representatives of all the major functions of the business. The committee formulates proposals for the approval of the chief executive. Although this can be highly successful as a method of planning for change, a committee is hardly the most efficient medium through which to implement changes. This phase of the exercise is still better controlled by an individual, and if the chief executive has the time he is the ideal choice since the more formal authority the individual possesses, the better.

In assigning individuals to the task of reorganization, perhaps the greatest consideration is the question of bias. In the early days of 'management games', referees were often surprised at the amount of heat generated in arguments about structure, though normally the determination of the organization structure was only one stage in the game and, by itself, relatively unimportant. We now recognize that the 'players' tend to do two things in these circumstances: to reproduce the structure of the enterprise in which they work and to place their own function or profession at as high a level in the organization as possible. A marketing man tends to hold it as self-evident that his company should be marketing-oriented. He has a built-in prejudice for a particular type of structure. Engineers, designers, accountants, etc., all hold similar *idées fixes*, even if subconsciously.

Many companies have found that an organization specialist from outside provides the solution to the problems inherent in choosing an 'insider' for the job. No doubt he will have greater knowledge of and experience in reorganization than the 'inside' part-timer. He will also find it easier to step back and view the company from a distance.

The Changes

The period of time over which structural changes are introduced, whether there is an overnight 'earthquake' or a gradual evolution of the improved structure, depends partly on the causes of the reorganization and partly on the company's attitude towards organization planning.

Companies that are large and sophisticated enough to have an executive or department with a full-time responsibility for organization planning and change, tend to regard reorganization as a continuous process, based on a constant, critical introspection. Plans are made for five or even ten years ahead, and these long-range plans are broken down into detailed reorganization targets. In such companies organization planning and manpower planning may be linked, so that sudden reorganizations are not forced on the company by the retirement of personnel.

Although specific cases will require specific treatment, a reorganization will involve the following: first, a survey of the present state of the enterprise and an analysis of its structural faults; second, a search for and choice of alternative structural arrangements; third, the 'installation' of the new structure; and finally, the proof of the benefits of the changes made.

In the first stage, the aim is to identify the characteristics of the existing structure, but not only of the structure. Even if the decision to reorganize were prompted by recognition of just one major organizational fault, we could not expect to diagnose the disease accurately by observing one symptom, however obvious. A doctor would want more evidence than a headache before diagnosing a brain tumour. We must first obtain an overall impression of the business, examining both structural and non-structural details.

An Analytical Framework[1]

Many people in an organization have ideas about what is wrong with it; many consider that they know just what sort of treatment should be prescribed for the company. Although the organization analyst will

[1] Although approached from a different viewpoint, this framework for organization analysis is not dissimilar to a scheme conceived by Pugh et al., see 'A Conceptual Scheme for Organizational Analysis', *Administrative Science Quarterly*, Vol. 8, No. 3, December, 1963.

hear these subjective opinions, he must get below the surface and discover facts, the 'law of the situation'. Only by examining every aspect of the organization, every process, every pressure on its activities, will he track down the causes of malorganization.

To take just one example, many companies have a particular structure as a result of the opinions and preferences of their founders, and they retain these formal structures long after the founders have ceased to be active executives and long after the structure itself has been outdated. Examination of structural factors alone, however detailed and concentrated, will not necessarily reveal the causes of the inefficiency; these are inbred – the result of history and tradition.

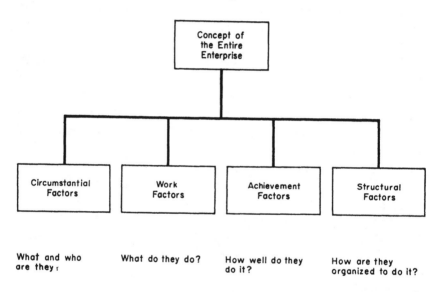

It is a commonplace that the circumstances in which different companies operate themselves vary. History and tradition are examples of such 'circumstantial factors'. Circumstantial factors consist of rather intangible factors which together help to answer the question 'who and what is this organization?' In more detail, they will include facts about the origin, history and traditions of a company. To discover these the analyst can examine the company's charter, its self-image, and in particular, any recent changes in policy, products, organization and control. Type of ownership is another circumstantial factor. Here the analyst is concerned with the amount of participation by the owners in the running of the company. The contracts of directors and their powers should also be considered under this heading. Size too is relevant, in terms of assets, capital, turnover and employees. Closely related to these are the locations and sites at which the company operates, and the types and sources of and constraints on the company's finances.

Under the heading of environment there is a further large group of circumstantial factors. What are the nature, size, product-variety, stability and fashion-consciousness of the market? What are the nature, size, strength, product-variety, substitutes and product-development record of the competition? What technology and skills do competitors have? What are the sources of supply of materials and human resources? What effects do national politics have on the business? What is the external culture, the social environment? Has the company any concern with patents, quotas, restrictive trade agreements or agencies?

There are also more domestic matters, such as the management: are they 'sleepers' or 'thrusters'? What is the predominant supervisory approach? Again, the degree of unionization should be considered; which unions are involved?; to what extent is there a closed shop? Finally the analyst should try to sense the general atmosphere by considering the welfare arrangements, fringe benefits, the degree of paternalism and the rules for behaviour.

A second category of differences are the 'work factors'. An examination of these will answer the question: what does this organization do? There are many examples of companies that started life as small, batch-production engineering concerns. Some of these are now large mass-production enterprises. It is not only the growth factor which necessitates structural change; recent research has indicated that companies of roughly equivalent size but with different types of production need different structures. Although the evidence for a direct correlation between structure and type of production is not yet conclusive, it seems likely that a refusal to change at least the method of controlling and supervising production along with a change in the type of production itself will lead to symptoms of malorganization.

Type of production (batch, continuous or mass) is only one work factor. The structure analyst will also need to investigate the main production processes, the preparation and assembly of components, if appropriate, and the finishing. What methods are used to control quality,

157

stock, production, cost, progress and credit? What are the main procedures, clerical, accounting, reporting, etc.? How does the company derive sales forecasts, order trends, and what is the system for determining order quantities for bought-in goods and equipment?

Personnel methods form another group of work factors. What attention is given to measuring management performances, and what are the criteria and standards? How is success rewarded? How is failure punished? What incentives are offered to motivate high achievement? How are training and development carried out at all levels?

Finally the analyst should consider the work factors related to the technology employed in the company. He will need to know the extent of automation in the factory and in the office. Is there a computer? What is it used for? What are its intended uses?

The third category of differences between companies has the title 'achievement factors'. These answer the question 'how well does this organization perform the tasks it sets out to perform?' Here again the links with organization structure can be extremely close ones. For example, companies that aim at certain targets in the product innovation or staff relations field may be frustrated if responsibility for the achievement of these targets is placed in the wrong hands.

To discover a company's achievement factors an analyst should consider the external image of the company, its status in the eyes of competitors and the general public. He must look at the market share of the company's products. Profitability should also be considered. What is the return on capital, the margin on sales? How do these compare with competitors? Are inter-firm comparisons available? How good is the company's record of product innovation – with regard to speed and percentage success?

Certain internal factors too can add to the analyst's picture of the company's achievement factors. What are staff relations like? How well are employees motivated? How high is their morale? How high is labour turnover? Absenteeism? What is the standard of physical conditions? How well does the company meet its own overall objectives?

The fourth category consists of 'structural factors'. Here the analyst is concerned with answering the question: how is this company organized to do its work and achieve the results it requires? Structural factors receive more detailed attention later in the chapter; here we will attempt to summarize the main points to be considered.

158

A starting point for the analysis of structural factors is the formal organization chart, if one exists; and the details of the matrix of schedules of responsibilities. The analyst also examines the extent of centralization and decentralization, both of the company as a whole and of individual units. He should try to gauge the degree of rigidity or flexibility, formality or informality, bureaucracy or lack of standardization in the structure. He can gain an initial impression from the amount of written procedures, job descriptions, etc.

The authority structure should also be considered. Here again an 'authority chart' may exist, but this will reflect the formal position which may be very different from the actual authority structure. In this context too, the analyst looks at informal groups and their power.

Other structural factors include the formal and informal flow of information, the degree of specialization, methods of co-ordination and plans and allowances for management succession.

This analytical framework, consisting of the four types of factors, can be used to obtain a more comprehensive picture of the present state of the company. It is also important in the case of many of the individual factors to consider whether the company has specific intentions for the future. Clearly the company will have targets or objectives showing its achievement plans. But also the analyst should not overlook the possible impact on structure of such changes as production technology, the intended use of a computer or the purchase of a new factory site.

The amount of detail investigated will depend largely on the scale of the proposed reorganization and the time available. A thorough examination of every aspect of the company's operations should be undertaken when major external changes, such as the change from a seller's to a buyer's market, or major internal changes, such as the introduction of a computer, threaten to have significant effects on the company as a whole.

Methods of Collecting Information

Often a great deal of the necessary information will exist in a readily obtainable form. Such documents as the Memorandum of Association, sales records, etc., will provide a useful basis. But each piece of information must be checked, first to ensure that it is the latest available, and secondly to see whether it is in fact a reflection of top management's

159

ideal or actual company practice. A chart, job-descriptions, procedural instructions may all exist, but the information they give about the structure may present a very different picture from reality. If we could measure authority in very precise degrees, we would invariably find that the authority actually exercised successfully by a manager was more or less than his job-description would imply. To confirm, elaborate and expand the formal picture presented by existing documents, other, more penetrative methods of information gathering are required.

Questionnaire and interview are the analyst's main tools of enquiry. The questionnaire is the quicker and less expensive of the two but has severe limitations. At its very worst the questionnaire method will uncover no more facts about the company than can be found in official documents. If there is no follow-up after the questionnaire, any difficulties of language or ambiguities in the questionnaire can produce a totally false or irrelevant impression. It is also difficult with a questionnaire to obtain all the information required. An open question at the end requiring the manager to give opinions or make suggestions rarely yields as much as the same question posed in a face to face encounter.

It is true that some faults are common to both the questionnaire and the interview. But it is also true that a skilled interviewer can overcome them more easily than a good questionnaire. An interview programme though more expensive and time-consuming can yield a great deal more information. In particular, it will enable the analyst to detect the atmosphere, the styles of leadership, the informal relationships and other, similarly intangible forces at work in the organization.

A third alternative is to combine questionnaire and interview methods and use the questionnaire as a framework for the interview, checking and following-up on doubtful or conflicting reports. In any case the formal, structured meeting with an executive should follow a plan similar to a good questionnaire.

The analyst will need to ascertain as a minimum the following facts about the executive in a detailed investigation:

1. His name.
2. His job title, department and division.
3. The location of his office.
4. The name and job title of his immediate supervisor.
5. The names and job titles of others to whom he reports.

6. The names and job titles of those who report to him.
7. The tasks that he is formally required to perform.
8. The tasks that he does perform.
9. The tasks that he is formally required to and actually does supervise.
10. The extent of his formal (and actual) authority in: (a) personnel matters, (b) policy-making, (c) expenditure, (d) decision-making, (e) methods, etc.
11. His formal and informal relationships with others.
12. Reports he should and does read and submit.
13. The standard procedures he is subject to and abides by.
14. Other facts, opinions and suggestions he feels are relevant.

Successful fact collection from interviews relies primarily on having a clear objective. The analyst should decide the benefit he hopes to gain from each interview. Does he merely want facts about the company or the people? Does he want impressions and opinions? Is he trying to sell himself, the need for change or the actual changes? Is he gauging reactions? The objectives will determine whether an interview needs to be heavily structured or informal, whether it should last five minutes or half a day. It will also help the analyst prepare his interview plan.

Other techniques can improve the efficiency of fact collection. As far as possible, facts and opinions should be obtained first-hand from the best source. Certainly second-hand opinions can be misleading, and even first-hand opinions need cross-checking. Differences of opinion and their sources should be noted with particular care, as should exceptions from normal practices, and their causes. The interviewer should not allow himself to get sidetracked from his prepared course, though this is not to say that he should prevent a manager from 'talking himself out', if this will achieve the objective. Nor should he at this stage make criticisms or hint at vast, unspecified changes being imminent.

All relevant and useful information should be noted during the interview and written up as soon after as possible. Methods of recording information about the structure are dealt with later, but here it is important to emphasize that in the process of gathering information for reorganization, the analyst himself must be 'organized'. He will not be able to carry all or even most of the information in his head.

Objectives – The Criteria

When he has gathered and sifted all the information, the analyst knows the facts about the company as they are; he must then proceed to ask the question: are they in fact as they should be? This type of analysis implies criteria or yardsticks against which the facts about the company can be assessed. By far the most important criteria are the company's objectives. To be able to judge the structure, therefore, the analyst must first know the objectives of the enterprise.

Clearly the objectives of concern in such an analysis are not to be found in the Company Charter or Memorandum of Association. They are not the traditions on which the Company was founded nor the more philosophical ideals, such as the preservation of private enterprise; nor even the more concrete aims of satisfying the public, giving a good service or improving the standard of living. The objectives that are relevant here are primarily arithmetic quantities, related to time and with any constraints clearly stated.

Profit and other financial objectives must be established. Under this heading the analyst may need to know targets for turnover, gross and net profit, share price and dividends. Special aims for items such as reduction in bank overdraft or acquisition of more funds should be considered. Marketing objectives are another large group. What is the target for increase in market share and for increase in actual sales? Are there any plans for price changes? What are the objectives for the launching of new products or the termination of outdated lines? Productivity or efficiency objectives should be established. What are the percentage increase in output and reduction in input expected for each department? The analyst should also determine the objectives in relation to personnel. What is the personnel expansion or reduction target? What are the targets for training and development of personnel?

The time-scale of objectives and the constraints on them are as important as the quantities themselves. The analyst must discover whether they are long-term, short-term, immediate or 'special' objectives, and to avoid confusion he should establish what these mean in terms of time itself. Is a long-term objective for a year ahead or ten years ahead? He must obtain clear statements of constraints. For example, is it the company's intention to increase turnover by x per cent without increasing indebtedness?

We can use these overall objectives to derive operational targets

162

for the main functions of the business, production, marketing, account-ing, etc. Then against these we can judge the suitability of the existing structure.

Drucker's Tripartite Analysis

Drucker's first requirement of an organization structure was that it should provide for business performance. As a result, he saw an effective organization for given circumstances as the outcome of a logical process in which the 'activities', 'decisions' and 'relations' necessary to achieve objectives were carefully analysed. The nature of this analysis constituted an advance in the practice of organization structure. For this reason, we have adopted this three-part analysis as a part of our diagnostic approach to organization analysis. We claim, however, that other structural features require detailed examination, such as the span of control and the information flow. Furthermore, we consider that the most logical and rational solution must undergo adaptation to allow for the *people* in an organization.

The aim of *analysing activities* is to determine what the company is doing to achieve objectives and whether these are the activities which are most likely to be successful. All the necessary activities should be adequately provided for in the structure. A company in a manufacturing industry may have departments labelled Production, Sales, Accounting, etc. But these are like empty bottles. The analyst must decide what goes into each; whether marketing, for example, includes sales and market research; whether these need to be separated; what is their relative importance in relation to the objectives.

Some functions which are traditionally regarded as part of other functions may need to be separated out to receive special attention.

Because conditions in the environment, in particular the needs of the market, are constantly changing, the traditional view that a company needs a stereotyped set of functions is an inadequate approach to activities analysis. No two companies are the same in every respect, so no two companies require identical activities, neither in type nor size. Nor are the activities determined as necessary to meet this year's objectives identical with those needed by the company to meet next year's objectives.

We should, therefore, carry out a thorough analysis of the company's

163

activities. Are they the ones most likely to achieve objectives? Which activities go together in the light of objectives? Which need to be separated out for special attention? What needs to be done that is not done at present? Are there any redundant activities? Are there any short-term activities which outsiders could perform more effectively?

In the *decisions analysis* we attempt to determine the level of management at which specific decisions are and should be made. There are four characteristics of decisions which can provide an indication of their importance and thus the level at which they should be made.

First, the importance of a decision depends on the degree of futurity in it. How long into the future does it commit the company? How quickly can it be reversed and what would be the cost? Secondly, the scope of influence of the decision should be considered. To what extent and at what level are other functions and departments of the business affected by the decision? Major changes in product design to solve manufacturing problems require the attention not only of designers and production men, but also representatives of the marketing function. Thirdly, the degree of subjectivity or qualitative factors involved affects the level at which a decision should be made. Does the decision require the man to make certain ethical, social or political assumptions and judgements? Decisions whether to hire handicapped workers or those who have served prison sentences would be in this category. Finally, the importance of a decision depends on the frequency with which it occurs. Is it repetitive, like reorder decisions? Is it common, such as the decision to recruit workshop personnel? Is it rare, like the decision to build a new plant? Or is it unique, like the decision to accept a takeover bid?

When all foreseeable types of decision (which should account for at least 90 per cent of all decisions) have been assessed along these four lines, the existing assignment of decision-making in the company can be analysed. We can ask of each type of decision: is it being made at a low enough level? Is it delegated close to the scene of action? Is it being made at a level which ensures that all affected functions and departments are considered? Is every decision formally assigned to someone? Have any been left to chance? Are the people capable of making the decisions delegated to them?

By analysing relations we aim to establish with whom a manager works, the contribution he makes to the work of others, and the contri-
164

bution others make to his work. The usual approach in defining a manager's relationship is to look primarily at those he supervises and decide the nature of his 'downwards' relationships. It is more important, however, to establish first the 'upwards' contribution he makes to company objectives, to consider his relationship to higher units. A quality control manager, for example, has the task of supervising the quality control department. But to say this does not establish his place in the overall structure. Is it more important that he reports to the production manager? Or is his function really to maintain the sale-ability of the product, and so should he be accountable to the marketing department?

Similarly, lateral relationships are determined by considering the way that individual targets combine to achieve overall objectives. It is not sufficient to establish formal relationships between production and sales on the one hand, and production and research on the other. All three should be formally related, if sales, production and research targets are to produce the profit objective.

Clearly, when analysing relations we should consider the people involved. Here, as with decisions analysis, the logical solution will need to be adapted to make allowances for the existing personnel.

Analysis of Other Structural Variations

The question 'is it appropriate for the achievement of objectives?' should also be asked of each aspect of the company's structure.

With most structural features it is a question of attaining the right balance between two extremes neither of which is absolutely desirable or undesirable. Is the degree of centralization or decentralization correct both overall and for individual groups of activities? Is there too much rigidity or flexibility? Is there the right balance between formality and informality? Are job descriptions, written procedures, etc., too detailed or not sufficiently detailed? Is there evidence of gross role overload or underload? Are spans of control and levels of management balanced correctly?

Authority and responsibility too require close examination. Is any function being performed without accountability for results? Where are formal and actual responsibility different? Is there evidence of Empire-building? Is it to the advantage of the organization? Has any

165

manager taken part of his previous job with him when he was promoted? Does this matter?

More general questions too should be asked. How well does the company respond to external pressures? Does it adapt or resist? How quickly does it hear of changes in the environment? How good is the information flow? Are the methods of co-ordination effective?

By these and similar enquiries, and by the analysis of activities, decisions and relations, we dissect the existing structure and diagnose the faults in the organization. We took as our premise for this exercise in logic the objectives that the company set itself. In the final section of this chapter, we hope to show that in practice company objectives are only one of a pair of premises, and that right from the start of a reorganization our thoughts should be guided not only by the objectives but by the requirements and abilities of personnel.

Analysis of the People

As a secondary objective of his interviews with executives, the analyst will be compiling assessments of their abilities, limitations, temperaments, etc. His analysis of the people in the company will be very different from his analysis of the activities, decisions, relations and structural variations. In practice, the analysis of people will indicate the constraints on the ideal structure envisaged as a result of the other analyses. In every case decisions will have to be made whether to engage new personnel or rearrange the tasks so that they can be performed by the existing personnel. With the latter solution, at least there is the advantage that the company has some idea of the abilities of the men.

People, unlike activities, cannot be split up and rearranged at will. They may be resistant to change; often they are simply unable to change. A man who has practised an authoritarian style of leadership for years will have great difficulty in adapting to a more permissive climate. Also, in this context, the existence of informal groups receives attention. They are notoriously resistant to change. Their strength may even be derived from outside the organization in some religious or political affiliation. They may be serving a purpose which requires formal recognition. The analyst should try to identify them, assess their strength and their contribution to the organization, both as they are and as they could be.

In the practice of organization structure we are dealing all the time with people. Of activities, decisions and relations it may be meaningful to ask whether they are as they should be. And if they are not, whether we can change them. People, however, are not so adaptable. Training can make up certain deficiencies, effective motivation certain others. Yet still we must recognize that people are not pegs that will fit perfectly into holes even after a little smoothing down, unless the hole takes into account the characteristics of the peg.

People, therefore, are to a large extent, like objectives, the datum of the organization structure. The new structure in practice, therefore, will not be less logical than the ideal theoretical structure. It we accept as our datum both the company objectives and the existing personnel, the most logical structure is one which achieves the company objectives while making best use of the personnel.

Chapter 14

Charts and Diagrams

Limitations of Organization Charts

An organization chart is a visual aid – a supplement to a verbal description of a structural framework. Charts are sometimes used as the only method of imparting information about the organization pattern and for detailing responsibilities. For the former, they provide an uncertain and vague appreciation of the general outline; for the latter they are wholly inadequate. The traditional chart shows job titles – Production Manager, Marketing Manager, etc. – which are but a poor reflection of the complex of duties attributable to each position. The traditional chart reveals little about the job of the Marketing Manager, except that it exists, that it is formally related vertically to a higher level and to a number of lower levels.

What can a well-drawn organization chart show? First, it details a collection of job titles and possibly the names of job holders – though a simple 'head count' could be more cheaply and clearly given in a typed list. It also shows the formal authority structure – who is nominally responsible to whom; but it does not show the nature of the responsibility. It may attempt to show rank but in most organizations ranks are not sufficiently clearly defined to allow unambiguous visual representation. However, a good chart will reveal in broad outline the structural base of the organization – whether it is product-based, market-based, function-based, etc.

An organization chart can have very real value to an organization analyst. He can use it first as a means of obtaining a broad impression of the existing structure – a form of shorthand, with references to more detailed written definitions of the responsibilities and relationships of which it is a reflection. He can further make use of the chart form to visualize alterations in the structural pattern and their general consequences.

Drawing Organization Charts

The organization chart is the most common of the types of chart for recording structural information. Its conventions are well established and its principles widely known. It is usually composed of a number of boxes, joined together as in Figure 1.

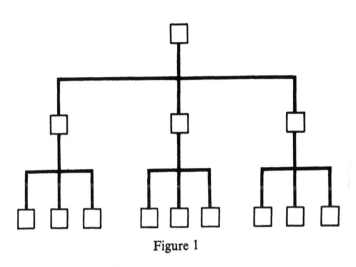

Figure 1

A number of simple rules and suggestions will greatly facilitate the drawing and increase the usefulness of such charts.

(i) For the analyst's purpose of examining the existing structure it is vital that he should attempt to portray the structure as it actually operates, and not as people believe it should or does operate.

(ii) Job titles should appear in the boxes, and if the names of job holders need to be shown, these should appear outside the boxes. Alternatively, both job title and name can be shown in the box, the former in capitals, the latter in lower case.

(iii) For clarity and reference, the chart itself should have a clear title, it should be dated and numbered, and it should carry a reference to any allied charts.

(iv) Again for clarity, the details should be well spaced. Supplementary charts can be used to avoid too much detail. If a chart shows only a part of an organization, open lines should be left to show this, as in Figure 2.

169

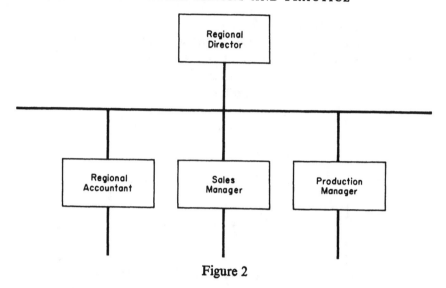

Figure 2

(v) It is usual to chart vertically, the most junior positions at the foot of the chart. Positions of approximately equal seniority may be drawn at roughly the same level. However, it is often difficult to reconcile the desire to present a neat, easily read chart with the need to show rank. When a chart is to be used to assist in presenting a new structure to the management of a company, it is advisable to include on the chart a note that 'The levels on this chart do not necessarily reflect the levels of the Management depicted.'

(vi) It is possible to vary the depth of boxes in an attempt to show rank. Even this cannot overcome the possibility that someone will object to being shown at a particular level; and charts which have a standard size box tend to have the advantage of neatness and clarity.

(vii) Difficulties can be caused by a lack of care when portraying deputies on an organization chart. Although, of course, the duties of a deputy cannot be shown in full, a differentiation should be made between:

(a) the Personal Assistant (Figure 3)

(b) the 'second-in-command' (Figure 4)

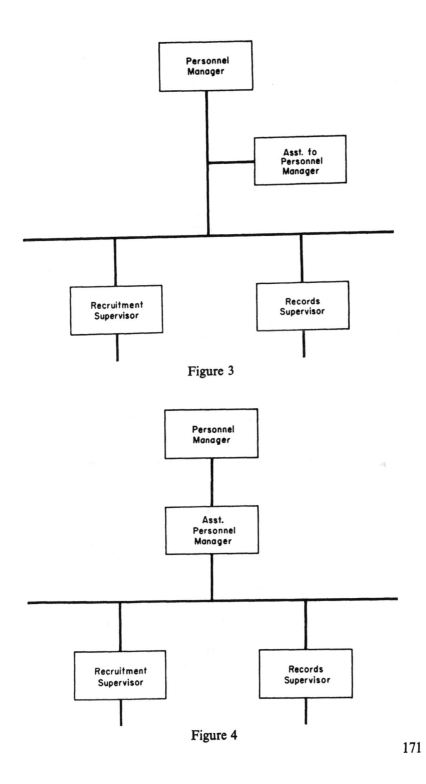

Figure 3

Figure 4

171

and the man who has responsibility for a particular group of people
(Figure 5)

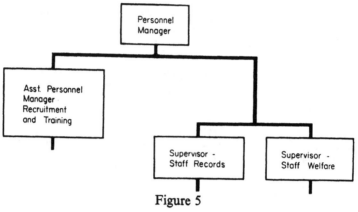

Figure 5

Other Types of Chart
There are several different types of chart which can be used to compensate for some of the deficiencies of the traditional organization
chart. Each one serves to illuminate just one or two specific structural
features.

1. Charts showing span of control and management relationships

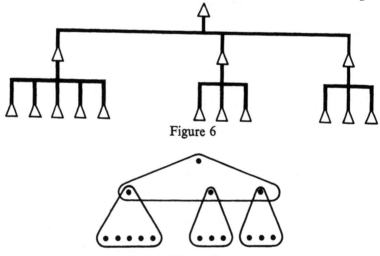

Figure 6

Figure 7[1]

[1] Adapted from R. Likert, *New Patterns of Management*, p. 105.

Figures 6 and 7 are frequently drawn, as here, without job titles or names. Figure 6 is a chart providing a visual representation of the spans of control in part of an organization. Figure 7 is a chart adapted from that on page 105 of *New Patterns of Management* by Rensis Likert. It shows both the levels of management and the vital relationships between groups of managers, every manager being a superior in one group and a subordinate or equal in another.

2. Authority Charts

An example of an authority chart, sometimes known as an A-chart or control chart, is shown in Figure 8.

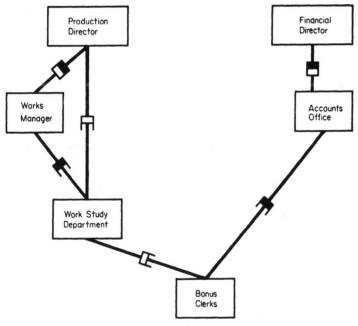

Figure 8

In drawing A-charts only three symbols are used:

indicates NOMINAL control and authority

indicates ACTUAL control and authority

indicates NOMINAL AND ACTUAL control and authority

The symbols are drawn so that the top is nearest the higher authority.

173

In some circumstances the A-chart will reveal little that cannot be discerned from the traditional organization chart. However, in gaining background information about the structure, the analyst will often find that the organization chart does not give a complete picture. People or a department may be nominally responsible to one person but in practice receive instructions from someone quite different. For example, Figure 8 indicates a possible weakness in the Work Study Manager's failure to assert himself.

3. Communication Charts

An example of part of a communication chart is shown in Figure 9.

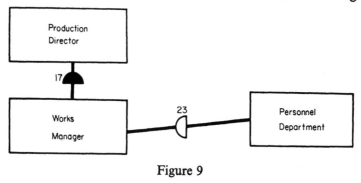

Figure 9

This chart is very similar to the A-chart. The symbols have the following meanings:

◗ – instructions given

◠ – information passed

The curved top of the symbol is nearest to the higher authority. The numbers on the chart refer to lists of the details of reports and instructions which are passed at each communication point.

The use of this chart tends to be more restricted than the A-chart. The 'information passed' symbol is often used for showing com-

174

munications between 'staff' specialists and 'line' operating managers, with the top of the symbol facing the 'line'. Since the 'instructions given' symbol virtually duplicates the function of the 'actual authority' symbol on an A-chart, it is recommended that the A-chart, with the 'information passed' symbol superimposed, should serve the purpose of showing both authority structure and communication network.

4. Profile Charts

Profile charts are used to describe in graphical form certain structural characteristics of an enterprise. The characteristics are isolated and a rating applied. A graphical representation is then drawn of the results as shown in Figure 10.

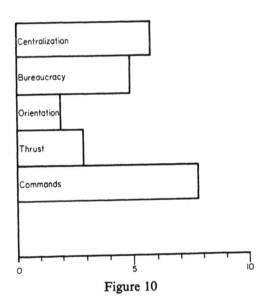

Figure 10

5. Admin. Flow Chart

An example of part of an Admin. Flow Chart is given in Figure 11. This chart shows the administrative procedures occurring during a specific management action. In skilled hands it can be used to uncover lack of delegation, rule by committee, etc. These symbols are used:

175

◇   DECIDE or Forecast

D   DELAY

▽   DIRECT, Command or Control

△   DELEGATE, Request, Motivate, Convince

○   DO, Act, Manage, Organize, Consider

⧡   PLAN

The time quoted down the side of the chart is calendar time (not work content) with 5 days = 1 week.

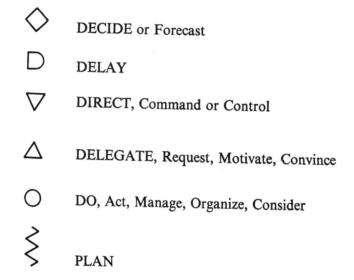

Description	Days	Plant Director	Sales Manager	Production Manager	R & D Manager	Accountant
1. Director suggests product		△1				
2. Considers request	1		○2			
3. Thinks about it	9		D3			
4. Decides; writes report	2		◇4			
5. Director looks at report	1	○5				
6. Thinks about it	4	D6				
7. Decides on further action	1	◇7				
8. Calls meeting		▽8				
9. Wait for meeting	5	D9				
10. Meeting held, decide to pursue	1	○10	◇10	10◇	10◇	10◇

Figure 11

Charts are a means, not an end. Of themselves, they have little value. However, as tools of analysis, as supplements to verbal communications, and as media for idea-selling, they can be most useful to the organization analyst.

176

Chapter 15

Designing and Installing a Better Structure

Little research has yet been specifically aimed at determining whether there is any arithmetic relationship between structure and success. Most writers, at least until very recently, have propounded management principles and theories drawn from experience of a very small sample of business enterprises. Personal reminiscences of this kind serve a useful purpose in illustrating specific management practice but they are individually an uncertain foundation for any general management theory. Management theory should only gain acceptance when it is reflected in widespread, successful management practice. What is needed is much more solidly-based research in this whole field.

It is necessary to emphasize that the recommendations in this chapter are only suggestions; they may need to be adapted (or even ignored) in a particular situation.

The Effects of Production Technology
Between 1953 and 1957 a team led by Joan Woodward studied the organization structures of industries operating in Essex. Although the area is comparatively small, a cross-section of industries and company sizes was examined such that certain generalizations from the findings would seem to be justified. Two important discoveries of this study were:

1. companies that were successful tended to have middle-of-the-road characteristics of organization structure (e.g. span of control)
2. there was a stronger correlation between structure and type of production than between any other variable (e.g. size).[1]

[1] J. Woodward, *Management and Technology*, HMSO, 1958.

Companies can be classified according to the methods employed in production. Ten categories can be arranged in order of increasing complexity of technology and then grouped into three larger overlapping divisions as follows:

Group I
Small batch and unit production

1. Production of simple units to customers' orders.
2. Production of technically complex units.
3. Fabrication of large equipment in stages.
4. Production of small batches.
5. Production of components in large batches subsequently assembled diversely.

Group II
Large batch and mass production

6. Production of large batches, assembly line type.
7. Mass production.
8. Process production combined with the preparation of a product for sale by large-batch or mass-production methods.

Group III
Process production

9. Process production of chemicals in batches.
10. Continuous flow production of liquids, gases and solid shapes.

Span of Control

The span of control of the chief executive widened considerably with technological complexity. In Group III companies it was wider than in Group II companies, where in turn it was wider than in Group I companies.

The span of control of the first-line supervisor, however, was wider in Group II companies than in either of the other Groups. Among the unit production companies the first-line span of control of successful companies was in the range 22–28; in mass production the range was 45–50, while in process production the range was 11–15.

Number of Levels of Authority
Here again there was an increase in line with technical advance. The median number of levels of authority for Group I was three, for Group II four and for Group III six.

From these details we can obtain the shape of the organization structure for each group. Successful unit production companies tend to be short and broad-based – a 'flat' type. At the other end of the scale process production firms tend to have a more 'pyramidal' type of structure – a tall and rather narrow-based. Mass production firms, on the whole, tend to be both broader and taller than unit production firms but not as tall as process production firms, the relative shapes being something like this:

GROUP I   GROUP II   GROUP III

Other Technology-related Characteristics
It appears that mass production firms have the most formal and rigid procedures. In successful unit and process production companies job descriptions, definitions of duties, etc., are less detailed. Communications are more often written than verbal in mass production firms; in the two other groups they tend to be verbal.

Functional specialization as a feature of organization was found to be more prominent in successful large-batch and mass production companies. In unit and process production few specialists were employed apart from those who had a direct responsibility for the production process; in mass production companies the traditional 'line-and-staff' pattern was more common with a split between the responsibility to produce and the responsibility to supply specialist assistance.

Only in the large-batch and mass production firms was there a relationship between adherence to traditional management theories and success, which is perhaps a reflection of the narrow experience from which many of these theories are derived. 'Outside these systems [i.e. large batch and mass production], however, it appears that . . .

179

an alternative kind of organizational structure might be more appropriate.'[1]

Bureaucracy

It is fashionable to condemn the bureaucratic type of organization. Certainly the contemporary emphasis on the people in an organization and the necessity of change and adaptation would seem to militate against the formality, rigidity and standardization which are the strengths of bureaucracy. Yet it cannot be denied that a bureaucratic organization has advantages, and may even be preferable in certain circumstances.

It should be given serious consideration wherever it is vital that rules are adhered to and that all duties are discharged irrespective of staff attendance. Non-industrial examples include essential services such as those provided by hospitals and prisons, electric power stations and gasworks. Parts of these enterprises may require an organization structure which is predominantly bureaucratic. Similarly in industry certain essential maintenance departments may need bureaucratic elements in their organization.

Job Descriptions

A precise and detailed description of jobs is a feature of bureaucracies; in certain cases, therefore, such descriptions will be needed, just as bureaucracies themselves are indicated in given circumstances. A formal and detailed approach to job description is also often indicated in large-batch and mass production companies.

In other situations, however, the use of very precise and detailed job descriptions should be carefully questioned. It will frequently be of greater value to provide instructions for operating machinery. Descriptions of tasks (rather than jobs) can be provided in the form of algorithms.

In companies other than those with bureaucratic structures or those engaged in large-batch or mass production, a good rule is that the length of a job description should be inversely proportional to the rank of the manager whose job is being described. For example, the manager

[1] ibid., p. 21.

of the Training department may have a job description four pages long; that of his superior, the Personnel Manager, may be only three pages long. When we get up to top management the job descriptions may be only a page in length, and the chief executive's only half a page – or does he really need one at all?

Divisionalization

Generally speaking, a divisionalized structure based on product groups will only be appropriate for the larger companies. The fact that each division should be large (and profitable) enough to support a separate management team prevents most of the smaller companies from benefiting from this more flexible and aggressive type of organization.

It is, however, indicated where the company is sufficiently large, and where the other conditions apply; namely, where production techniques for the products are diverse and/or where there is a distinct market for each product.

Product Innovation

Two major requirements for successful product innovation are: creative, well-equipped researchers and a structural arrangement oriented to the search for and development of new products. The innovative skills of the researchers should be directed to market needs. Sales and production personnel should be involved in the commercialization of laboratory developments.

Basically the problem is one of co-ordination between Sales, Production and Research. There are several possible answers, all of which have proved to work in practice. The simplest solution is to appoint a General Manager who is not oriented towards any one of the three functions but rather to the objective of satisfying the needs of the market. Another solution is to establish what amounts to a separate company to handle each new, commercially viable idea. A third solution is to set up cross-functional, co-ordinating teams of committees. If these operate at a low enough level it avoids the problem of which Follett complained, of having to patch together finished webs.

181

General Managers

The General Manager is increasingly emerging as a useful organizational concept. He has been introduced successfully as a short-term expedient and also as a long-term structural feature to fulfil various purposes. In the short term, a General Manager can bolster up a team of weak functional managers, or supervise the integration of a new function, or fill the role of 'trouble-shooter'. In the longer term, he can relieve the chief executive of part of his burden and help to reduce his span of control where this has become too large. The introduction of a General Manager to co-ordinate functional operations has been mentioned above, and the need to fill this role increases as, in many industries, the number of functional specialists increases.

Working Parameters

The analyst is working within many parameters:

- those factors given in this chapter above (and other more advanced ideas)
- principles, etc., of organization (given in Chapter 17).
- the objectives of the enterprise.
- the strengths and weaknesses of the enterprise.
- the threats and opportunities offered by the environment.
- the people working for the enterprise.
- experience.

Within these parameters, various possible solutions evolve. These solutions will be based upon the following stages:

- what activities and functions are needed to satisfy the objectives?
- which of these activities and functions are the major ones?
- how should the activities and functions be grouped?
- what should the hierarchy of activities be?

- what, in outline, is the division of work between the executives in charge of the major activities?

- are any of the major activities to be so poorly headed that the overall performance of the enterprise will be seriously reduced? Should the executive concerned be replaced or not, and if so by whom?

- what are the characteristics of the new structure? (e.g. amount of decentralization, nature of co-ordination, degree of formality, rigidity, standardization, size of spans of control, interdependence, relationships of 'staff'.)

- in each main activity or function, how should the sub-systems be allocated for maximum effectiveness? Is every activity covered?

- how should decision-making (e.g. capital, personnel) be allocated between the various groups and levels?

- are there any potential personality or people problems? Will the retirement pattern cause difficulties in the near future?

Testing Solutions

The various solutions are charted by the analyst. In practice, this results in a series of charts each with a particular emphasis or in anticipation of particular opportunities. There are various ways of preparing these charts. Some people draw charts on translucent gridded drafting sheets; a chart can be copied (by dye-line), altered, recopied and so on. Other people use pieces of card about one inch square on which are written names of people or sections or tasks or departments or functions, etc. These can be mounted on plastic with double-sided adhesive tape, photocopied, realigned and so on.

It is impossible to 'try out' a series of organization structures in an enterprise and then pick the best one. So a Test Programme is undertaken before installing a structure. This testing takes the form of examination, costing and simulation:

Examination

The new structure is checked as though it were an existing structure by the methods quoted in Chapter 13. This examination is better carried

183

out by a person other than the originator and who may do so as part of the 'simulation' approach (see below).

Costing

The differences that a new structure will make are costed. In practice, it is found that it is not possible to put a figure readily to everything. Instead, the analyst quantifies what he can (e.g. staff costs, accommodation) and lists those items that are unquantified. With practice, it is found that most items can be quantified for purposes of comparison.

Simulation

Under simulation, a new structure is treated as though it actually existed; four possible testings are:

- brainstorming. A brainstorming session is held at which a list is prepared of all the things that can go wrong with the new structure.

- role-playing. Two or more people 'act out' particular situations as they would arise between two or more members of a new structure.

- devil's advocate. A person is given the task of 'proving' that a new structure is inferior to the existing one.

- In-tray. An analyst has to act as though he were an executive in a particular position within a new structure. An In-tray is given to him which contains a number of problems. These problems must be tackled within the context of the organization being considered.

It is only by mentally 'attacking' a new structure in these ways that an analyst can feel confident that it is correct.

Installing the New Structure

It sometimes happens that a large enterprise, with a record of labour troubles, can introduce radical changes without upset: yet a small concern, with comparatively good labour relations, may face bankruptcy as a result of trying to introduce just one manager from outside.
184

The problems of practical reorganization are the human difficulties of accepting and adapting to change. Very many organizations, by their nature, are resistant to change. We have seen in earlier chapters that the traditional view considered the very strengths of an organization lay in its ability to defend itself against the effects of external changes, to stand erect and face the storm rather than bend with it. To carry through a successful reorganization, the positive benefits of bending with the storm should be emphasized rather than the dangers of resistance.

What are the specific fears and difficulties that people may experience during a period of reorganization? People commonly find a new role unsuited to their temperament. Two jobs which require the same basic training may call for totally different personalities. A case in point is the company that transferred to its Work Study department the task of clerical work organization and methods. In many cases the change would have worked, since the skills required by the study staff for both types of work are very similar. In this particular company, however, the change was an unfortunate decision; the approach that suited the male workers in the machine shop was not effective with the girls in the office. The skills were adaptable, the study-men's personalities were not.

Practically everyone in an organization is affected by a change of structure; other types of change tend to have more localized effects. People sometimes feel, rightly or wrongly, that a change in structure – even in a distant part of the company – is adversely affecting their status or prospects of promotion. The less obvious the need for the change, the more sinister its intent appears to be. A change in the main activities can cause difficulties, especially if it has been established by the activities analysis that a previously high-level activity is of less importance than its position in the structure indicated. To the head of such an activity there can be no compensation for demotion.

A change in the formal structure may threaten an informal structure which has developed and grown in strength over a long period of time. It is often the nature of such groups to resist change except those changes which further their ends. Resistance may come from an informal group not only because they find the changes unacceptable but simply because, amidst all the changes taking place, their case or even their existence has been ignored.

The human problems of reorganization are not so much solved but

185

avoided by anticipation. The attempt to understand people's needs and temperaments, in addition to assessing their abilities, is a step in the right direction.

Many of the problems arising during a reorganization can be overcome by detailed planning, correct timing and pre-selling the idea of change. Even in the initial stages of investigation the analyst should be attempting to create a climate in which people will discuss things willingly, openly and frankly. Objections should be uncovered in these early stages rather than at the time when changes are actually taking place. Even when they have accepted the changes in theory, people will still take time to adapt to them in their work. And the phasing-in of the new structure will need, in many cases, to be a gradual process.

To be accepted the new structure must have a number of obvious, unarguable advantages over the old. Often, for example, the advantages of more decentralization are clear, and top executives are relieved to have a lighter burden. But it should be remembered that however logically sound the new structure and its benefits for all, there will still be a minority with whom the analyst will need great skills of persuasion.

As a final point on the mechanics of reorganization, the process of introducing and implementing changes should never be allowed to lose momentum. The planned programme of changes should be continued at a steady pace and with an increasing sense of inevitability.

The Proof

The new structure will be judged by the results of the reorganization. It will be judged, first, by considering whether the company's objectives have been achieved. Another test of its success will be the extent of disruption of operations in the company. Were deadlines achieved, output maintained, costs held, backlogs prevented and quality upheld? Finally the success of the reorganization will be judged by the attitudes and atmosphere in the company. Is the company poised ready for the future? Is morale high? Management enthusiastic?

If there is an affirmative answer to all these questions then the structure is right – for the present.

Chapter 16

Case Studies

It is instructive to see how the ideas in this book have been applied in practical situations by consultants operating assignments for clients. A few case studies have therefore been chosen to illustrate various aspects of Organization Structure.

The examples have been chosen for their interest rather than any other reason. To avoid repetition, only the first case study describes the whole approach.

REORGANIZATION OF AN ELECTRICITY BOARD

The investigation of the operations and organization of 'D-board' provides a detailed illustration of the complete process of organization planning for a large commercial enterprise. The implementation of the proposed structure will not be complete for some time, but the processes of fact-finding, diagnosis, prescription and planning for implementation illustrate many of the important principles and theories discussed in the text.

Fact-finding

The first task was to discover the facts about the Board and its operations. The fact-finding process was based on:

- Interviews; nearly one hundred members of the staff were interviewed.

- Data, published both internally and externally, relating to the Board's activities.

187

- Published reports on the development of the relevant part of England and discussions with the Regional Economic Planning Council.
- Visits to all areas, a selection of districts and other of the Board activities.
- Internal information and analyses, specifically prepared for the investigation.
- Internal reports, forecasts and plans.
- Information provided by PA specialist services on:
  - computers
  - market research
  - personnel
  - work for other Boards, the Electricity Council, other fuel boards and other public bodies.

One group of facts deserves particular attention; these concern the Board's objectives and policy which necessarily have a direct effect on the subsequent organization structure.

Objectives and Policy
The Board's overall objectives were:

1. To provide an electricity supply and service at a level which satisfies the statutory requirements.
2. To achieve the stipulated return on investment.

The two most significant ways in which the return on investment could be improved were to increase the surplus or reduce the net assets. At the time of the investigation an efficiency-raising programme (aimed at reducing labour cost and hence increasing the surplus) was being carried out, However, it seemed unlikely that the overall cost reduction would have more than a marginal effect upon return on net assets. The other approach seemed to offer more; a significant improvement in the return on net assets could result from a reduction in assets relative to the volume of electricity sold. To achieve this the following objectives were stated:

188

– to obtain a better demand curve.

– to be more effective in planning and controlling the process of reinforcing the network for peak demand.

This approach was particularly relevant since:

– the distribution assets accounted for nearly 90 per cent of the Board's total assets.

– the distribution network must be designed to cope with peak demand although this may occur on only a few occasions each year.

– more precise methods of forecasting peaks for each part of the network would have a significant impact on investment in distribution and generating equipment.

– the cost of increasing the ability to cope with peak demand would be enormous.

The two functional areas of the Board's operations which could have the most direct effect on the achievement of these overall objectives were marketing and engineering. Policy in these areas was therefore the subject of detailed examination.

Marketing Policy
It was decided that the marketing function could make its best contribution by operating according to a policy defined as follows:

– to reduce fluctuations in the load curve by encouraging consumption outside the peak and by discovering consumer habits and appliances which contribute to the peak.

– to sell as much electricity as possible within these conditions.

Such objectives required an aggressive marketing organization and had an important effect on the proposed structure.

189

Engineering Policy

The key engineering decisions were related to reinforcement and extension of the distribution system, and on these decisions depended capital investment of some millions of pounds.

In the light of this policy and the sums of money involved any improvement that could be made in the forecasting of demand peaks could have a substantial effect upon the scale of investment needed. The existing system of forecasting was based on historical data and would be invalidated by an aggressive implementation of the proposed marketing policy.

The Existing Organization

Though the Board had successfully tackled many of the problems of growth over the twenty-year period since its establishment, the nature of the task of certain organizational units had changed considerably and they were no longer suitably constituted for their new role. Certainly, to achieve the redefined objectives, a better organizational plan could be developed. Specific faults observed in the existing organization structure included:

1. *Authority and Responsibility not adequately defined*

   There was an inadequate appreciation of the delicate relationship between specialists and 'line' managers. It was possible for a 'line' manager to obstruct changes, based on Board policy, for a number of years.

2. *Decisions by Committee*

   Possibly as a result of (1) it was difficult to define decision points and consultation across the major functions of the business was necessary. In consequence a large amount of management time was occupied by committees (nearly 500 committee meetings at various levels in a year) and decisions tended to be a group rather than an individual responsibility.

3. *Interpretation of Policy*

   A result of decision by committee in the existing organization was the difficulty in obtaining interpretation of policy. For example there were sixteen possible courses an enquiry from a district clerk could take to get an answer at Board level.

4. *Management Appraisal and Development*

The divided responsibility of most positions tended to inhibit effective management appraisal and development.

5. *Communications*

The long lines of communication (particularly from district to H.O.) made it difficult to act quickly. Some attractive sites for shops may have been lost as a result of the delay in getting a decision from H.O.

6. *Lack of Informal Communication*

There was a strict observance of protocol despite the length of formal channels. Matters which were generated by the lowest organizational units and were known to require H.O. approval, nevertheless had to receive consideration at each intermediate level. There was in some units a feeling of remoteness from H.O.

7. *Lack of Marketing Flexibility*

Despite the degree of autonomy given to District managers, who were mainly engineers, there was a lack of flexibility in choosing a marketing approach to local conditions.

8. *Dual Responsibility*

Both the creative and operational aspects of particular functions were often carried out by the same manager. A new marketing development, for example, would be interrupted frequently with queries or advice requested by the field sales force. Although this has aspects which in other circumstances would recommend it, such an arrangement was not conducive to the generation of creative marketing which was a central feature of future policy.

9. *Difficulties of Co-ordination*

There was inadequate provision for the co-ordination of inter-functional or inter-departmental proposals, particularly in developing new marketing packages.

10. *Information and Control*

There was a lack of a co-ordinated approach to computer system design. This resulted in the development of individual programmes within a function, with little regard to the method of integration with other users. An overall system outline had not been prepared.

191

Most of the existing control information was based on comparative data rather than standards. This tended to focus attention upon the reasons for differences rather than upon commitment to achieving a target.

This lack of effective control information inhibited delegation to lower levels of management.

Objectives of the Proposed Structure

To correct all the possible faults of the existing structure would have resulted in the design of an impracticable ideal. Priorities were therefore established and as a result it was decided that the new structure should as far as possible satisfy the following requirements:

- it should be as simple as possible in terms of levels of command and the functional units within the levels.

- there should be a split between creative and operational activities both at Board level and within each function.

- creative and policy responsibility should be with the chief officer in each case while operating responsibility should lie with his deputy.

- creative and planning activities should be centralized, while maintaining effective communication with operational units.

- operating responsibilities should be delegated as far as possible down to the local unit.

- all points of customer contact should, if possible, lie within the commercial sphere of control.

- lines of command should follow the predominant pattern of communication, whether single or multi-functional.

The Proposed Structure

The Functional Approach

It was proposed that the new organization structure should have a basic subdivision by functions and that the normal line of command should

192

be functional rather than multi-functional. The top-level structure, therefore, is shown in Chart A.

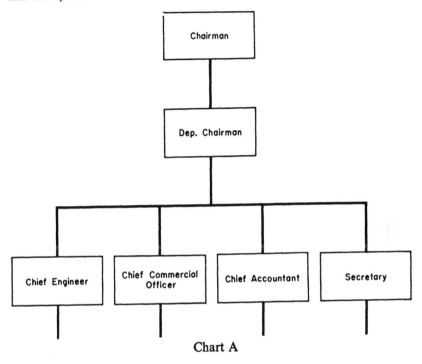

Chart A

In the case of this Electricity board the arguments in favour of such a functional split were strong:

- in a technically based industry, there is a need for decisions to be made on up-to-date specialist information.

- D-board is a large organization, but homogeneous; based on one 'product' and concentrated in a relatively small area.

- the normal flow of communications within the enterprise is functional rather than cross-functional.

- the number of levels and size of units are not necessarily the same for each function.

- the two main activities – selling and distributing electricity – were already organized on a functional basis.

193

Policy and Operational Activities

A second outstanding feature of the proposed structure was the clear separation of policy-making from operational activities. This was felt to be especially desirable in order to:

- prevent policy decisions being unduly inhibited by operating difficulties.

- allow concentration of effort on policy creation.

- identify responsibility points more clearly.

- speed operational decisions.

- allow different frequencies of meetings for policy and action.

The resulting separation is seen in Chart B which again shows the top level, together with the second level. The *block* lines are used to identify the two elements of policy creation and action, as indicated on the chart. The chairman, chief officers and one group co-ordinator have a responsibility for policy creation while the deputy chairman, deputy chief officers and two group co-ordinators are responsible for operations.

This separation is also clearly reflected in the organization within each function. Chart C shows part of the commercial organization. Here we can see that the chief commercial officer is responsible for 'marketing' while his deputy is responsible for 'selling'.

Other Aspects – Evaluating the New Structure

Clearly such a major reorganization could have been the subject of a whole book (the final report to the Board consisted of over 130 pages of text and 19 charts, maps and tables). The details, however, of schedules of responsibilities, size of units, methods of co-ordination, are not relevant here; but it is relevant to answer the question whether the proposed structure was a significant improvement on the existing organization.

After careful analysis and comparison of the two structures, the following advantages were recognized in the new structure:

194

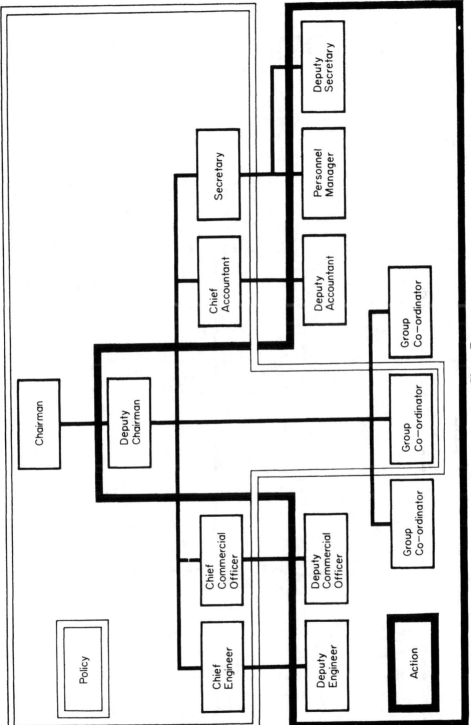

Chart B

COMMERCIAL

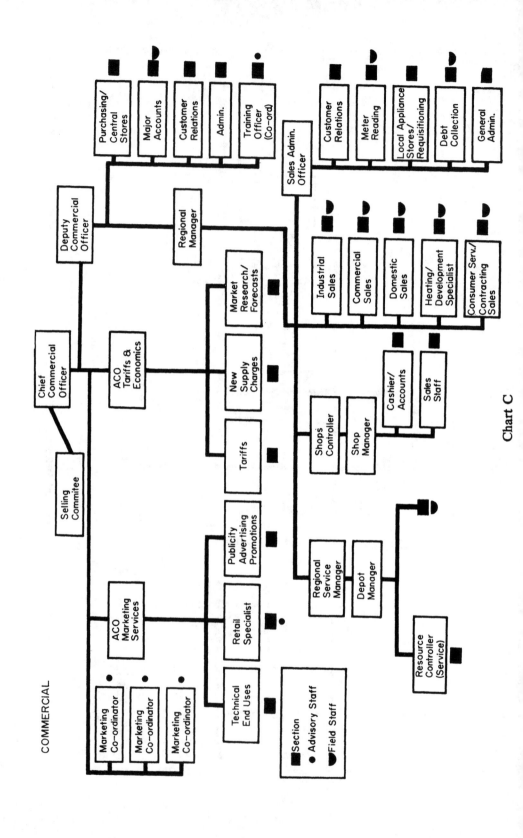

Chart C

– a better customer service as a result of the concentration of customer contact in the commercial function.

– a more effective implementation of policies, particularly within functions.

– quicker management decisions, reduced decision by committee, better management development and career opportunities, better management control as a result of the shorter lines of command and communication.

– more scope and time for creative thinking as a result of the clearer identification of responsibility for this activity.

– better use of specialized management and technical skills as a result of the functional approach.

All of these should contribute to higher morale and a better return on investment.

MARKETING AND PRODUCT INNOVATION IN A MANUFACTURER OF HEATING EQUIPMENT

Consultants were engaged to look at the strategy of this company in the light of its objectives of growth and continuing independence. Far from growing, the company was found to be declining. This, it was felt, was mainly the result of two factors:

– product innovation was slow, mistimed and misdirected.

– new products were designed with a view to ease of production rather than with an eye on the market.

Organizational features and management practices appeared to be at the root of the trouble in that insufficient attention was given to either the marketing or the innovation aspects of the business. Particular faults were:

– there was no definition of responsibility for these functions (in fact, there appeared to be little formal structure at all).

197

- there was no marketing function.

- the information systems were inadequate.

- management development and control were virtually non-existent.

To remedy this situation it was proposed that the operational activities of the company should be delegated to three divisions based on the products they made. Each divisional manager had a clear profit responsibility for the operation of his division. Policy and planning, on the other hand, were centralized at group headquarters. Three new functions were created for the group as a whole; these dealt with economic planning, technical planning and research and development. These, too, were centralized to ensure that they received sufficient attention.

DECENTRALIZATION IN A PUBLIC BODY

Another public body, with a very large area, engaged consultants to examine the possibility of reducing the number of district offices.

The existing organization provided for twenty-six district offices, all reporting directly to Head Office. Very little autonomy was allowed to district offices and control was centralized at Head Office. In an enterprise where reaction and adaptation to local conditions were important, the ability to do so was severely inhibited by the established structure and procedures.

The proposed organization consisted of only five district offices, covering larger areas. Head Office functions were to be decentralized wherever possible. The results of the change were:

- a smaller H.O.

- decision-making in most matters was made locally.

- there was a better local service to the public.

- all contact with the public now went through the district office.

- district staff were more conscious of profitability.

- district personnel gained greater experience of general management and consequently were more promotable.

198

GROWTH AND DIVERSIFICATION IN CONFECTIONERY

Many companies are experiencing change as a result of growth. One such client had overall objectives and profit plans which were not practicable in its existing main stream of activities, manufacturing and retailing confectionery. Experience in controlling a chain of retail outlets had been satisfactory and the company had a good supply of expertise in this area. Diversification was recommended into retailing of toys, being a growth area and comparatively unexploited on a specialist chain-store basis.

The existing organization structure was thought to be unsuitable both for this venture and for the general objective of growth. The main features of the structure were a strong personal control by the chairman and a very informal allocation of responsibilities and chain of command. This had had strong advantages for the small, tightly-knit company, but was not conducive to growth. The disadvantages were:

- lack of initiating by middle managers who had no clearly defined authority.
- lack of control of factory supervisors.
- need for top management to be involved in detail.

It was felt to be particularly important that any change in structure should, therefore, meet these requirements:

- a clear profit responsibility for separate activities.
- delegation of detailed operations leaving top management free to plan and manage change.
- central provision of services to operating sections.
- provision for management succession.

The basic feature of the revised structure was the setting up of two separate divisions, one to handle the manufacturing of confectionery, the other the retailing of confectionery and toys. Within the retailing division itself there was to be a split between confectionery retailing, toy retailing and property acquisition and management. This would

199

help to ensure that the growth area of the company's activities received sufficient management attention. Furthermore, top management are freed from day-to-day operational control by the introduction of departmental managers in the factory and the two operating managers controlling confectionery districts and toy districts. The accounting and secretarial functions were established as centralized specialist departments.

REORGANIZATION OF COMMITTEES IN A LOCAL AUTHORITY

Views on committees vary considerably but their existence is inevitable in local government. One local authority, in whose reorganization consultants were concerned, revealed the following facts about its use of committees:

- there were 14 committees in existence.
- Council members also sat on 19 external committees.
- standing committees had a membership of 27.
- other committees averaged 10 members.
- on average councillors were members of seven internal and three external committees.
- three members were each on 16 committees.
- some 1,200 hours of members' time was spent on committees in a six-month period.
- trivial matters often occupied hours of discussion.
- senior local government officers often attended long council meetings while matters concerning them may only have occupied a few minutes.

These facts about the committees are by no means untypical. The organization proposed and installed is illustrated in outline in Chart D opposite.

This chart shows the structure to have three basic elements, excluding the Council itself; the management board, the committees and the clerk

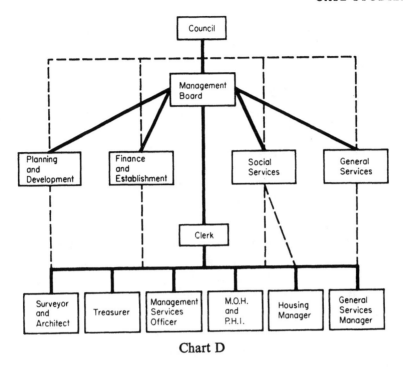

Chart D

and chief officers. The management board, a structural innovation, had the following functions:

- to formulate the principal objectives of the authority and present them to Council for decision.

- to review progress and assess results on behalf of Council.

- to maintain overall supervision of the organization, co-ordination and integration of the authority.

- to take decisions delegated by Council which exceed the authority of chief officers.

- recommend decisions to Council where authority has not been delegated.

The committees, reduced to four in number, had these functions:

- to make recommendations to Council via the management board

201

on the major objectives of the authority, and study and recommend means to attain these objectives.

– examine new ideas.

– review progress on plans and programmes.

– consider any matters raised by their own members or referred to them by the management board.

– consider the interests, reactions and criticisms of the public and convey them to the officers and, if necessary, to the management board.

The clerk was to be responsible to Council via the management board for the efficient management and execution of the authority's functions. All chief officers and heads of department were to be responsible to the clerk for the efficient and effective running of their departments.

This new structure and distribution of responsibilities had the following advantages:

– the committees no longer need be concerned with routine administration nor with taking executive decisions.

– no councillor need serve on more than two committees.

– members could spend more time with electors.

– each member had a higher status and his work became more interesting and significant.

NEWSPAPER OFFICE

The organization chart of one department in a newspaper was as shown in Fig. 1 opposite. For various reasons (including considerable extra work undertaken by the Financial Accountant) the span of control was too large. The work was therefore divided into two main logical groupings: (a) day-to-day operating of accounts, and (b) more academic accounting functions. The final organization (including two changes of title) was as shown in Fig. 2.

This selection of case studies demonstrates both the wide variety of situations encountered and the need for individual answers.

202

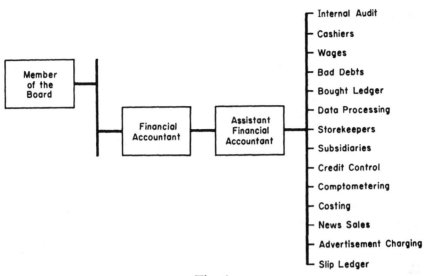

Fig. 1

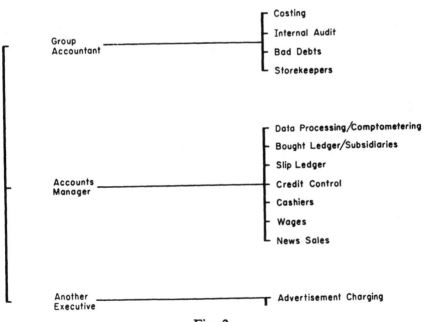

Fig. 2

203

Chapter 17

Principles and Maxims

Sixty years ago Henri Fayol, in many ways ahead of his time, put forward his fourteen Principles. One of these was the dogmatic assertion: 'Centralization, like division of labour, is one of the laws of nature.' Later writers supported ideas such as 'one man, one boss' and 'the ideal span of control is four'.

However, during this century business, industry, commerce and affairs of state have all become much more complex. This has led to Principles becoming modified.

The Principles given below will be considered as true by the majority of Organization Structure specialists. They are not trivial however – they would not have been postulated in their present form sixty years ago, nor are they all necessarily acceptable to every manager and director.

Principles of Organization Structure
1. The objectives of the enterprise and its component elements should be clearly defined, agreed, and known.
2. The organization structure should never be regarded as permanent. It needs to remain flexible and to be reviewed periodically.
3. A structure should recognize the personalities and the people to be included.
4. The Chief Executive has the ultimate liability. It is not possible to deprive him of his accountability, his authority, or his responsibility as to what to delegate.
5. The real reasons for reorganizing must be known and the major pressures behind the reorganization clearly identified.
6. Decentralization is normally desirable and can be achieved by

delegating the right to take or initiate action closer to the scene of action. A measure of centralized co-ordination and control should be used to prevent unilateral actions incompatible with overall objectives.

7. Activities and functions should be grouped according to homogeneity of objective and the purpose they serve.
8. In any situation there is a limit to the number of positions that can be effectively supervised by a particular individual. This number should be kept at a maximum consistent with optimum effectiveness.
9. The number of levels of authority should be kept to the minimum consistent with optimum effectiveness.
10. A superior is accountable for the acts of his subordinates. Accountability should be coupled with the level of positional authority.
11. Controls, systems and procedures can be more effective than job descriptions and organization charts in installing and maintaining a structure.
12. An organization is only as good as the people within it, and is a reflection of those people. Therefore, for an organization to develop, it must in turn develop those people within it.

Maxims

These maxims each contain in a few words a basic truth about Organization; they frequently express a reservation about the wholehearted acceptance of a common principle or idea:

THE ATTAINMENT of size does not of itself guarantee success. If success is measured by any normal quantitative yardstick, dis-economies of scale can, and sometimes do, set in.

DECENTRALIZATION has its own positive advantages. It is not simply the result of bad communications or information flow.

'IT TAKES more than the structural design of an organization, however, to ensure sound management. No organization is sounder than the men who run it and delegate others to run it' (A. P. Sloan, *My Years with General Motors*).

MANAGEMENT by Exception may not be enough – if the need for periodic audit is ignored or if the initial conditions are wrong.

205

MANAGEMENT by Objectives may not be enough – if the need for motivation and incentive is ignored, or if Organizational slack is allowed to develop.

VARIED and high-powered Staff is not a perquisite of affluence but a prerequisite of success.

MANAGEMENT can be tough-minded and abrasive in its dealings with competitors without necessarily having an Autocratic structure. Of the three archetypes of Autocratic, Participatory and Democratic structures, the one to be preferred is Participatory.

TOO MANY levels of organization keep the top men too far from the firing line. This can frustrate active executives by denying them sufficient working contacts.

SOMEONE, somewhere, is rejecting our favourite principle of organization and still being successful; but this in no way diminishes the need for us to abide by our principles.

Chapter 18

Conclusion

We have come a long way since Moses. The simplicity of his solution matched the simplicity of his problem and of his time. Our problem may be basically the same but is more complex out of all proportion. The need for the organization of the People of Israel could be accepted because it could easily be shown to be of benefit to them all. The dangers from outside the organization accentuated the need to group together and organize in order to survive. For us the need for security and survival is less often such a direct stimulus to action; but when we are forced by pressures from outside to realize that our survival can be threatened, things appear to run more smoothly inside. On the whole organizations seem to perform better in a competitive environment. The moral here is not that we must have competition and external pressure before we can expect organizations to function well, but that a great part of this phenomenon is a result of the acceptance, by the people in an organization, of its ability to help in satisfying their own need for a measure of security. The personal need for security and survival in such circumstances reverts to being an active motivator rather than a mere dormant factor. It is conceivable that, if the people in organizations today could more often see their membership of the organization as a means of satisfying their most strongly felt needs, those organizations would be more effective and successful.

This is just one reason why Moses' situation was different. The essence of his problem was the same as ours, but the solution must be different for us, since our needs are different from the needs of the People of Israel.

Is not, in any case, the word 'solution' rather glib in this context? Our present state of knowledge is such that we cannot draw decision trees showing a completely logical answer to a given problem of

207

organization. This may, however, be the direction in which we should be progressing – since research has revealed that certain organizational variables can be correlated.

The reader of this book may be motivated by a general interest in the subject; his interest is indeed welcomed since the greater the number of people who realize the complexity of the organization-planner's problem, the more sympathy there will be with his task. It is more likely, however, that the reader is a student of organization and management, either a manager, an in-company management trainee or a business school undergraduate. The needs of these groups differ, at least in emphasis, but we have tried in this book to cater for them all.

The student, it is hoped, will benefit from this book as a mountaineer would from photographs and maps before an expedition. He can rapidly survey the subject, see the snags and areas of controversy and dispute, examine briefly the approaches that others have made. All these investigations will help him to form his own approach – his own personal concept of organization. He can then proceed to other books, such as those listed in the bibliography, knowing how they fit into the literature as a whole, knowing where their authors stand, and, therefore, better able to evaluate their contribution.

The practising manager too can gain similar benefits from this book but for him organizational problems are often more urgent and time in shorter supply. He will want the writer on organization to show how a structure can be designed and made to work more effectively. It used to be felt that a manager could be given a set of valid and generally applicable principles to hang on the wall of his office. This is no longer considered (by most theorists) to be possible, since organizations consist of people and people do not conform to general rules and principles. Many improvements can however be made in specific cases, and the investigation process, described in detail in Chapter 13, can benefit managers greatly in highlighting the specific needs of their situation.

Although it is difficult to conceive of generally-valid rigid principles of organization, this book has tried to convey a number of messages; some of these are about organization, some about people in organizations and some about organizing.

The importance of objectives is a message which has been implicit in almost every chapter and every topic discussed. Why are we in business? This question should be the starting point of the organizing process. What are the overall objectives of our organization? What should our operating objectives be in the long term, short term and immediate future to achieve our overall objectives? The answers to all these questions should have a substantial effect on the design of an organization structure, and the evolution of that structure in practice. Objectives are both the starting point of the organizing process and the end which the process helps to achieve.

Another important message concerns the extent to which we can measure how well objectives are being achieved. We should be able to judge how we are progressing in relation to the plans that we have made. The structure should contribute by allowing measurement of performance, adjustment and correction. It must highlight weaknesses in their early stages. The main result of this emphasis has been the concentration in this book on the merits of establishing profit centres which are meaningful and so making the accountable manager easier to identify.

The third message has been about the need for flexibility of structure. An essential ingredient of business success is the ability to recognize and exploit or even create opportunities. Drucker went so far as to say that the primary objective of a business is to create a customer. Since the second world war we have witnessed in this country the growth of direct selling from manufacturer to consumer, of launderettes, of super-markets, of manufacturers of vegetable, mineral and chemical by-products. In each field, the opportunity was recognized by an enterprising few. The ability to see the opportunity requires insight and 'flair' – qualities of good management. The ability to profit from the opportunities requires speed of reaction, flexibility, an absence of red-tape – qualities of a good organization structure. This has led to a number of companies aiming to be not so much the best producers of a particular range of goods nor the best satisfiers of a particular market, but essentially the best exploiters of profitable opportunities and growth areas.

The fourth message emphasizes the subject of people in organizations. Throughout this book we have attempted to show the effects that certain types of structure can have on the people who have to work within them. It would not be an exaggeration to say that by far the most common cause of failure of 'good organization principles' has been

209

their unacceptability to the majority of people to whom they are applied. To take just one example, from the many quoted previously: it is said that efficiency is greatest when specialization is the basis of division of labour. This, in theory, may be true; and in practice, it can work. Yet where the desire for efficiency by greater specialization leads to a structure based on function, rather than products or markets, the effect has often been to encourage empire-building and the search for high standards of professionalism within a function, rather than high standards of business performance aimed at achieving the objectives of the business as a whole.

The most important message about the people in organizations which this book has attempted to convey is the knowledge that everyone brings certain personal needs to his work and that with the majority of people effort is only stimulated by the realization that in this way a need can be satisfied. At the present time it is often found to be all too difficult to satisfy the *people* while achieving the objectives of the *organization*. What tends to happen is that they are frustrated by the organization with the result that they consciously or otherwise sabotage its achievement of objectives. An integration of needs is called for and a greater faith that such integration is possible. After all, what do people want? What do your colleagues and friends expect from their jobs? In most cases people can only be given what they want by giving the organization what it needs to achieve its objectives; and similarly the organization will lose if it does not satisfy those who work within it. A large number of people do not work particularly hard – an equally large number do not enjoy their work. Often the two coincide. Making the job more rewarding, not just financially, but socially and psychologically rewarding is more than half the answer.

When discussing the impact of people on organizations, we have emphasized the importance of groups. The idea that people work most effectively in isolation can no longer be supported, if it ever could. Only rarely and in a very small minority of occupations, has it proved to be an efficient arrangement. It is no longer merely a question of tolerating informal groups, but of instilling and strengthening group spirit of a pro-organization type, so that the whole is greater than the sum of its parts. The key phrase is Likert's: 'supportive relationships'. The boss does not abdicate his decision-making responsibility, but he realizes and accepts that the work of his subordinates is vital to his

210

success, and the subordinates for their part realize and accept that their fortunes depend very largely on the success of the whole.

This introduces the question of leadership. In most respects leadership is an attribute of management rather than of organization, but it has been discussed in this book, especially in Chapter 11, since the supervisor/subordinate relationship is such a vital link-pin of the organization structure. Much has been written in recent years about the superiority of 'participative' over 'directive' leadership. Certainly the nature of authority in business organizations is such that direction and control would not appear to be the best methods of exercising it; the realization that, for effectiveness, the decisions must be accepted as good decisions by the subordinates, means that they must acknowledge the superiority of the decision-maker, not just of his authority. Participation, therefore, increases involvement and commitment to the decision taken. But participation is not the same as democracy; nor should decision-making in industry ever become a completely democratic process, since speed and spontaneity (and, therefore, opportunity) are lost, if a manager must hold a referendum before any action is taken. And if he does this, can he be truly said to be a 'manager'?

Again people have an effect on the organizing process; we must take account of their reluctance, and often their inability, to change. We must above all win their support for the changes that are planned. There is a need for more consultation before changes are introduced.

Finally we come to the question of bias. In Chapter 1, it was stated that beliefs and ideas about organization are uniquely personal – we all have our own approach. In this book there are many theories with which we, the authors, would disagree. Yet they all have their place since someone, somewhere, at some time has used them with success. Who would have thought, for example, that Taylor's idea of 'functional foremanship' would be an effective technique in modern business conditions? We all have a bias – we all have our own set of concepts, but these alone should not prompt us to praise or blame. Praise and blame are only deserved by success or failure. No one would praise a company that followed the books and consistently made a loss.

What of the future? It is not easy to make valid predictions about future trends in organization structure. In the 1950s some organization theorists were predicting that the widespread use of computers would lead to greater centralization and the elimination of middle management. Neither has happened yet; but this is not to say that they cannot still happen. It seems quite certain, however, that enterprises will continue to grow on a corporate basis. Increased size with diversification spreads the risks and enables the enterprise to have a stronger bargaining position in financial matters.

At the same time, it is conceivable that companies will find it necessary to check the growth or even reduce the size of operating units. Any organization, whether a business unit, a charity, a sports club or whatever, has to grow beyond a certain threshold or break-through size which makes its operations viable (and, for the business unit, profitable); it must achieve critical mass. Many business units have, however, grown far beyond their critical mass, with the result that they can become inflexible and difficult to control; thrust has been lost, and so has the ability to exploit opportunities. Smaller operating units within even larger corporate organizations would seem to be one formula promising success for the future.

The most useful research in the future will tend to be along two lines. Personal reminiscences and individual case studies serve a purpose, but only a minority of companies will be in a similar enough situation for the same solutions to be effective. More research is needed of the kind carried out by Woodward in this country and Stieglitz in the United States, among others, comparing organizational variables in a number of companies and attempting to relate them to success. The second direction of useful organization research provides a fitting finale for this book – research about people in organizations. It is confidently predicted that the more we know about people's needs and abilities, the better equipped we will be to design more effective organization structures.

Appendix I

The Literature

Organization Structure and related subjects have proved a fertile field for writers over the years. It would serve little purpose to attempt a complete in-print bibliography. Instead three lists of books have been prepared in descending order of importance.

LIST A

This is a basic list of books recommended to anyone who wishes to read further about Organization Structure:

E. F. L. Brech, *Organization: the Framework of Management*, 1965

Cooper, Leavitt, and Shelley, *New Perspectives in Organization Research*, 1964

P. F. Drucker, *The Practice of Management*, 1955

H. Fayol, *General and Industrial Administration*, 1916

B. M. Gross, *The Managing of Organizations*, 1965

Katz and Kahn, *The Social Psychology of Organizations*, 1966

J. A. Littèrer, *Organizations: Structure and Behaviour*, 1963

J. A. Litterer, *The Analysis of Organizations*, 1965

March and Simon, *Organizations*, 1958

J. G. Marsh, *Handbook of Organizations*, 1965

H. F. Merrill, *Classics in Management*, 1960

National Industrial Conference Board, *Top Management Organization in Divisionalized Companies*, 1965

Sir W. Puckey, *Management Principles*, 1962

H. Sherman, *It All Depends*, 1966

H. Stieglitz, *Organization Planning*, 1965

J. Woodward, *Industrial Organization and Practice*, 1965

LIST B

This list contains the titles of some of the better-known books written on Organization Structure within the last 40 years:

C. Argyris, *Integrating the Individual and the Organization,* 1964
C. Argyris, *Personality and Organization,* 1957
E. F. L. Brech, *The Principles and Practice of Management,* 1953
Burns and Stalker, *The Management of Innovation,* 1961
E. Dale, *Planning and Developing the Company Organization Structure,* 1952
P. F. Drucker, *Concept of the Corporation,* 1960
Edwards and Townsend, *Business Enterprise: its growth and organization,* 1958
M. Haire, *Modern Organization Theory,* 1959
HMSO, *Management of Local Government,* Vol. I, 1967
H. G. Hicks, *The Management of Organizations,* 1967
R. Likert, *New Patterns of Management,* 1961
J. W. Lorsch, *Product Innovation and Organization,* 1966
Mooney and Reilly (Mooney, rev. ed. 1947), *The Principles of Organization,* 1939
J. O'Shaughnessy, *Business Organization,* 1966
E. Penrose, *The Theory of the Growth of the Firm,* 1959
Pugh, Hickson and Hinings, *Writers on Organizations,* 1964
Rubinstein and Haberstroh, *Some Theories of Organization,* 1960
Shultz and Whisler, *Management Organization and the Computer,* 1960
Simon and Barnard, *Administrative Behaviour,* 1956
Simon, Smithburg and Thompson, *Public Administration,* 1950
H. Stieglitz, *Organization Structures of International Companies,* 1965
Trist, Higgins, Murray and Pollock, *Organizational Choice,* 1963
L. Urwick, *Organization as a Technical Problem,* 1933
Sir G. Vickers, *Towards a Sociology of Management,* 1967
A. Zaleznik, *Human Dilemmas of Leadership,* 1966
Zaleznik and Moment, *Dynamics of Interpersonal Behaviour,* 1964

LIST C

This list represents a wide range of books on Organization Structure. It is not intended to be exhaustive but includes the majority of those titles likely to be mentioned by managers.

Alexis and Wilson, *Organizational Decision Making,* 1967
Alford and Beatty, *Principles of Industrial Management,* 1951
L. A. Allen, *Management and Organization,* 1958

J. Argenti, *Corporate Planning: A Practical Guide*, 1968

C. Argyris, *Executive Leadership*, 1967

C. Argyris, *Understanding Organizational Behaviour*, 1960

C. Babbage, *On the Economy of Machinery and Manufactures*, 1832

E. W. Bakke, *Bonds of Organization*, 1967

M. Bannerjee, *Business Organization: An Introductory Analysis*, 1964

C. Barnard, *Functions of the Executive*, 1954

B. H. Baum, *Decentralization of Authority in a Bureaucracy*, 1961

W. G. Bennis, *Changing Organizations*, 1960

Bethel, Atwater, Smith and Stackman, *Industrial Organization and Management*, 1950

Blake and Mouton, *Managerial Grid*, 1964

Blau and Scott, *Formal Organizations*, 1962

K. Boulding, *The Organizational Revolution*, 1953

Brech and Urwick, *The Making of Scientific Management* (3 volumes), 1949

British Institute of Management, *Organization Structure of Large Undertakings*, 1949

W. B. Brown, *Exploration in Management*, 1960

California University Institute of Industrial Relations, *Organization Theory*, 1962

Carzo and Yanouzas, *Formal Organizations*, 1967

Cohen, Dill, Kuehn and Winters, *The Carnegie Tech. Management Game*, 1964

C. Colston, *Management, Organization and the Team Spirit*, 1952

Comrey, Pfiffner and High, *Factors Influencing Organization Effectiveness*, 1954

E. Dale, *Organization*, 1967

H. Dennison, *Organization Engineering*, 1931

G. Drain, *The Organization and Practice of Local Government*, 1967

Edwards and Townsend, *Studies in Business Organization*, 1961

E. T. Elbourne, *Fundamentals of Industrial Administration*, 1947

A. Etzioni, *A Comparative Analysis of Complex Organizations*, 1961

G. G. Fisch, *Line-staff is Obsolete*, 1961

P. S. Florence, *The Logic of Industrial Organization*, 1933

Ginzberg and Reilly, *Effecting Change in Large Organizations*, 1957

Gulick and Urwick, *Papers on the Science of Administration*, 1937

HMSO, *Staffing of Local Government*, 1967

J. G. Hutchinson, *Organizations: Theory and Classical Concepts*, 1967

E. Jacques, *Organization for Overseas Marketing*, 1968

E. E. Jennings, *Anatomy of Leadership*, 1960

E. E. Jennings, *The Executive*, 1962

215

A. Lepawsky, *Administration*, 1949

K. Lewin, *Field Theory in Social Science*, 1951

T. Lupton, *Management and Social Sciences*, 1966

G. McBeath, *Organization and Manpower Planning*, 1966

D. McGregor, *The Human Side of Enterprise*, 1960

L. H. Matthies, *Organization as a Base for Systems*, 1966

H. B. Maynard, *Handbook of Business Administration*, 1967

Miller and Rice, *Systems of Organization*, 1968

F. G. Moore, *Management Organization and Practice*, 1964

N. P. Mouzelis, *Organization and Bureaucracy*, 1967

Mumford and Banks, *The Computer and the Clerk*, 1967

National Industrial Conference Board, *Growth Patterns in Industry*, 1952

National Industrial Conference Board, *Organization of Staff Functions*, 1958

N. Parkinson, *Parkinson's Law*, 1958

Petersen and Plowman, *Business Organization and Management*, 1948

Pfiffner and Sherwood, *Administrative Organization*, 1960

L. W. Porter, *Organizational Patterns of Managerial Job Attitudes*, 1964

W. Puckey, *Organization in Business Management*, 1963

Pugh and Hickson, *An Empirical Theory of Organization Structures*, 1960

F. M. Reza, *An Introduction to Information Theory*, 1961

Scott and Irwin, *Organizational Theory*, 1967

Seashore and Bowers, *Changing the Structure and Functioning of an Organization*, 1962

R. Stewart, *The Reality of Management*, 1963

F. W. Taylor, *The Principles of Scientific Management*, 1911

J. D. Thompson, *Comparative Studies in Administration*, 1959

J. D. Thompson, *Organization in Action*, 1967

V. A. Thompson, *Modern Organization*, 1961

H. Townsend, *Scale, Innovation, Merger and Monopoly*, 1968

L. Urwick, *The Elements of Administration*, 1943

L. Urwick, *The Golden Book of Management*, 1956

K. K. White, *Understanding the Company Organization Chart*, 1963

W. H. Whyte, *The Organization Man*, 1956

F. J. Wright, *The Evolution of Modern Industrial Organization*, 1954

B. Yuill, *Organizational Principles for Management*, 1966

Glossary

This glossary contains many of the terms encountered in the study of Organization Structure. Some of the words have other meanings in other disciplines or contexts; some words have more than one shade of meaning even within the context of Organization Structure.

This glossary will be found useful when reading the literature. When words are used with meanings different from those given, the author will usually indicate the sense in which they are to be used.

A

Accountability	The obligation to produce results, in terms of objectives achieved. Often associated with a profit centre.
A-Chart	Common contraction for Authority Chart (q.v.)
Adaptive Control System	One which continuously adapts itself to a changing environment by monitoring its own behaviour and automatically adjusting its parameters towards optimum performance.
Adaptive Sub-System	See Sub-System.
Admin. Flow Chart	A chart of the administrative procedures which occur in a managerial activity.
Articles of Association	The rules and regulations which specify the mode of conducting the business of a limited company. A model set of articles (Table A) is annexed to the Companies Act and this is often used by small companies.

Authority Positional authority – the status or standing of a person which depends on his position or office.
Sapiential authority – the status or standing of a person which depends on his knowledge or wisdom.
Charismatic authority – the status or standing of a person which depends on his personality and reputation.

Authority Chart A diagram of the nominal and actual authority and command existing in an organization.

B

Bureaucracy An organization based on laid-down systems, procedures, and laws in which any position is more important than the person holding that position.

C

Cascade An interconnected chain of groups of people in which the output of one group is used as the input to the next.

Centralization Raising the level in the hierarchy at which exists the authority to take or initiate action.

Channel An established path along which communications can flow.

Charismatic Authority See Authority.

Chief Executive The individual in whom resides ultimate authority, responsibility and accountability for results and actions.

Classical Theory A generic term for most of the theories of organization which appeared before 1920. Typified by H. Fayol.

Closed System See System.

Committee Theory The theory that tasks can be handled

by groups of interlocking committees rather than by individuals.

Communication Chart A diagram of the flow of information and instructions within an organization.

Conglomerate A group comprising subsidiary companies which do not have any obvious activities in common.

Critical Mass The concept that many human activities will not achieve a breakthrough if the quantities involved are too small, that is, smaller than the critical mass.

Cybernetics The study of control and communications in man and the machine.

D

Decentralization Lowering the level in the hierarchy at which exists the authority to take or initiate action.

Delegate To entrust to a subordinate the authority to take or initiate action, this authority to be subject to recall by the superior.

Democratic Theory The theory that all employees should have an equal say in running an enterprise (e.g. setting objectives).

Departmentalization (i) The theory that the organization problem is that of allocating tasks to people in such a way that most value is obtained.
(ii) Dividing an enterprise into units by function (rather than by product, area, etc.).

Div-Dec Shortened form of Divisionalized-Decentralized (q.v.)

Divisionalization Dividing an enterprise into relatively autonomous units. This term is usually reserved for those situations

219

when the division is by product, operating unit, region or customer (rather than by function).

Divisionalized-Decentralized An enterprise in which the activities are grouped into divisions and in which authority is decentralized to these divisions.

Division of Labour Allocating the total work load that has to be performed into small specialized elements. The aim is to divide people's work into a smaller number of tasks, so that they will become better at performing them.

E

Economic Man Theory The theory that it can be assumed people will make rational, logical, money-based decisions which are for their own maximum good.

Elaboration Natural tendency towards growth in the number and size of sub-systems (e.g. Parkinson's Law).

Equifinality Ability of open systems to reach the same result by different paths and from different initial conditions.

F

Federalism Type of organization in which separate divisions form a unity but remain autonomous in certain defined internal affairs up to a pre-set level.

Feedback Information returned from the output side of a system to a point nearer the input side.

Functional Foremanship System of first-line supervision (formulated and installed by Taylor) in which each subordinate received instructions from eight specialist supervisors (e.g. speed boss, route boss, repair boss).

G

General Executive   An individual who co-ordinates several functions without being part of any of the functions.

General Systems Theory   The theory that differing types of systems such as molecular, biological and social have certain common properties which can be applied to organization structures. Also that certain laws of heat, light, statics, dynamics (etc.) have analogies in organization structures.

Glacier Theory   The theory that the best approach to organizational relationships is one involving precise definition of jobs, methods and relations (this phrase has other meanings in other fields).

Greenfields   A situation where the enterprise (company, division, Ministry) has as yet no physical being.

Group   A number of individuals capable of being regarded as a collective unit. Command group – basic, formal, organizational unit consisting of a superior and his immediate subordinates.
Primary group – basic unit of a personal, close, intimate group, often voluntary in membership. There is disagreement in the literature as to whether or not this includes working groups.
Secondary group – a group in the membership of which an individual is valued for his contribution to the group's objectives. Task group – formal organizational unit of a group engaged on a particular task.

221

Group Dynamics A generic term for those techniques of group psychotherapy aimed at modifying inter-personal relationships and/or organization structure. Techniques include t-groups (q.v.), Grid Seminars and Psychodrama.

H

Hierarchy of Needs Concept that human needs can be arranged in ascending order and that satisfaction at one level is followed by desire for satisfaction at the next.

Holding Company A company which owns a controlling interest in other companies but which normally does not interfere in the running of those companies.

Holism (i) It is difficult to infer the properties of the whole just from a knowledge of the parts.
(ii) Dealing with the overall whole; regarding the elements as unknown or irrelevant.
(iii) Complete and self-contained systems are natural; part systems are not and are only found accompanied by stress.
(This word appears in the literature but is not attractive.)

Homeostasis A steady state, achieved by dynamics and not statics.

Hygienic Factors A form of incentive that does not of itself have a stimulating effect but which cannot be withdrawn without a disincentive effect. Thought to be necessary to maintain a climate in which Motivators (q.v.) will work.

I

Indian Theory Another name for Committee Theory (q.v.).

Industrial Democracy	General term for those techniques aimed at increasing employee participation and profit-sharing. Often localized to enterprise in which employee works.
Information Overload	See Overload.
Invisible Hand Theory	The theory that if people are rational in pursuing their own interests, then, other things being equal, the organization as a whole will benefit (from Adam Smith).

J

Job Description	A statement of the content and requirements of a job.
Job Evaluation	A generic term covering methods of determining the relative worth of jobs.

L

Laissez-Faire	The theory that there should be as little definition of managerial duties as possible.
Leading Sub-System	See Sub-System.

M

Machine Theory	The theory that organizations should simulate machines for optimum efficiency.
Maintenance Sub-System	See Sub-System.
Manage	To co-ordinate, plan, organize, motivate and control the work of subordinates.
Managerial Grid	A diagram (from Blake) with two axes – 'concern for people' and 'concern for production'. This is based on the assumption that the two axes of human-centred and task-centred styles are not dichotomous but can be maximized simultaneously.

223

Matrix A table in a specified order of rows and columns.

Matrix Organization A method of gaining entrée by a central staff expert to a decentralized department. Staff are assigned directly to these departments and maintain connections (functional or professional) with the central staff in their own specialities.

Memorandum of Association The document which sets out the objects for which a limited company is formed, and the conditions under which it is incorporated.

Merger The combining of two or more enterprises (companies, Police Forces) into one single enterprise.

Motivators Incentives that have a direct effect towards stimulating a desired action. Cf. hygienic factors.

N

Noise An unwanted fluctuation or signal in an information channel which carries no intelligence and which obscures the wanted information.

O

Office A position with a title in the official organization structure; the title is usually an indication of rank.

O & M = Organization and Methods A generic term for those techniques which are used in the examination of clerical, administrative and management procedures and organization in order to effect improvement.

Open System See System.

Order The concept of a place for everyone and everyone in his place (has other meanings in other fields).

Organization Chart	A diagram of the formal relationships existing between the various offices in an organization.
Organization Man	An employee who submits willingly and blindly to whatever the enterprise demands of him.
Organizational Equilibrium Theory	The conditions under which an organization can induce its members to continue their participation (and hence assure organizational survival). The theory that people balance what they get out of work (money, status, rewards, etc.) with what they contribute (time, worry, discomfort, etc.).
Organizational Slack	(i) Those activities in an organization that are directed at satisfying individual (or group) desires rather than the objectives of the organization. (ii) Over-manning of departments to enable management to meet organizational objectives more easily.
O.S. = Organization Structure	The way the hierarchy in an enterprise is structured.
Over-Definition	An over-precise definition of duties; so precise that it leads to conflict between the demands of various duties or to rigidity on managerial activities.
Overload	Over-work due to the office itself and not to the person holding that office. Role overload – an excess of legitimate calls from more than one person upon the time of an office-holder. Information overload – an excess of information for processing or interpretation.
Over-Ride	To retain ultimate control without being concerned with details.

225

P

Participation	Determination to a certain degree by people of their targets and methods of working.
Posdcorb	An acronym for the work of the executive based on Planning, Organizing, Staffing, Directing, Co-ordinating, Reporting and Budgeting (from Gulick).
Positional Authority	See Authority.
Power Equalization	The concept that each group should have equal access to information on every topic.
Profile Charts	Generic term for diagrams showing specified characteristics of an enterprise, normally on a quantitative scale.

R

'Responsibilities' Tasks for which a person or group is responsible:
(i) an obligation to answer to a superior for the successful carrying out of delegated activities.
(ii) the activities, function or work assigned to a particular individual or group; the state of having these assigned.

Retrenchment A major economy or cut-back in the size or scale of activities of an enterprise.

Role (i) The part a person is expected to play.
(ii) In structure analysis it is almost equivalent to a group of activities or one of the elements of an office.
(iii) In sociology it is almost equivalent to status.

226

Role Ambiguity   The situation where the behaviour expected of someone in a particular role is vague or has not crystallized (e.g. staff).

Role Conflicts   The situation where the actions expected of someone in a particular role are clear but contradictory.

Role Overload   See Overload.

Role Performance   How an individual who occupies a particular position behaves (compared with how he is expected to behave).

Role Theory   A generic term for those theories stating that certain norms of behaviour are expected of people occupying a particular position.

S

Sapiential Authority   See Authority.

Self-Actualization   An individual's continuous process of achieving his full potential. Self-fulfilment.

Situation (The Law of the)   Circumstances alter cases. A principle originally put forward by classic writers to answer the criticism that their other principles were too cut and dried (from Follett).

Sleeper   A manager (or enterprise) who is defensive, apathetic, negative, static (cf. Thruster).

S/N Ratio (Signal/Noise Ratio)   The ratio of desirable to undesirable information in a channel (e.g. a rumour has a low S/N ratio). Information Theory holds that the S/N ratio can only be improved by time-consuming methods such as filtering or the integration of several repetitive signals.

227

Span of Control The number of subordinates under the nominal control of a superior.

S.P.I. Standard Practice Instruction. A step-by-step description of how the administration and/or clerical work is to be performed.

Square-Cube Law Theory The theory that as an enterprise grows, there is a linear relationship between the square root of 'outside' employees and the cube root of 'inside' employees (from the Mathematical theories of Organization). 'Outside' employees are those in contact with outsiders (e.g. buyers); 'inside' employees are those who rarely meet people from outside the enterprise (e.g. production). This phrase has other meanings in other fields.

Stranger Laboratory A group (of say 20 people) from a variety of occupations come together for several days. During most of this time they are divided into sub-groups (called t-groups) for work. The object of a t-group is to enable its members to observe and learn about personal and group behaviour and relations. The staff trainer is absolutely permissive, is open, honest about his personal feelings and does not attempt to interfere with the proceedings of the group.

Structure Manner of organization; arrangement of parts.

Structure Analysis The technique of examining management procedures and organization in order to effect improvement.

Structured Laid out in a definite manner, planned.

228

Sub-Goals   The objectives of an organization can be split up into smaller contributory objectives called sub-goals which are assigned to individual groups.

Subsidiary Company   A company in which the parent company holds more than 50 per cent of the voting power.

Sub-System   A generic term for the subdivisions of the whole enterprise, e.g. department, branch. (This word has other meanings in other fields.)

Leading sub-system – the sub-system which can exert most pressure on the activities of the whole enterprise.

Supportive sub-system – one that procures the input and disposes of the output (e.g. Purchasing and Sales).

Maintenance sub-system – one that is responsible for maintaining the status quo (e.g. recruitment, indoctrination).

Adaptive sub-system – one that provides feedback from the environment (e.g. Market Research).

Supportive Sub-System   See Sub-system.

Synergy   The power of several groups working together to produce disproportional results, the whole being greater than the sum of the parts; often expressed as $2 + 2 = 5$.

System   (i) The method of performing paper or administrative work.

(ii) A complex group of connected things or parts.

(iii) The whole enterprise.

Closed system – one that is self-contained.

Open system – one that is in constant contact with, and is affected by, its environment.

T

T-Group See Stranger Laboratory.

Theory X and Theory Y Two concepts of human attitude (from McGregor). Theory X says that people dislike work, have little ambition, want security and must be made to work by external control. Theory Y says that people will learn to accept responsibility, that work is as natural as play and that one can rely heavily on self-control and self-direction.

Thruster A manager (or enterprise) who is aggressive, opportunity - searching, positive, dynamic (cf. Sleeper).

Top Management Those managers reporting directly to the Chief Executive.

Top Management Information System A structured procedure for collecting, storing, processing and disseminating all the data and information required by management from a single data bank. A computer-based concept, normally.

U

Uncertainty Absorption This occurs when inferences are drawn from a piece of information and the inferences (rather than the information itself) are then communicated. The recipient of this communication is then severely limited in his ability to judge the correctness of the original information.

Unity of Command The concept of one man, one boss.

Unity of Direction   The concept of one head and one plan for a group of activities having the same objective.

W

Weber's Law   If a salary structure is to have a uniform incentive value then the salary levels of an organization should increase in geometric proportion.

Index

233

self-formed groups, 124
Simon, H. A., 53–56, 88, 147, 213, 214
simulation, 184
Sloan, A. P., 205
Span of Control, 15, 46, 48, 54, 78–81, 172, 178, 205, 228
specialization, 16, 24, 31, 45, 48, 60, 76, 77, 105, 179
'staff', 45, 49, 57, 104, 179, 206
Stalker, G. M., 142
standardization, 24, 56
Stieglitz, H., 212, 213, 214
superior/subordinate relationships, 16, 34, 36, 38, 39, 48, 58, 79–80, 104, 127, 173, 205
system, open, 22, 26, 27, 63, 230
closed, 26, 27, 67, 229
Systems Approach, 26–28

t-Groups, 148, 228
Tannenbaum, R., 129, 149
'task' groups, 124–125, 221
Taylor, F. W., 30–32, 33, 216
Theory X and Theory Y, 56–57, 136, 230

Unity of Command, 24, 33, 46, 54, 104, 230
Urwick, L. F., 23, 44–47, 63, 129, 214, 216

Weber, M., 35–37
Weber's Law, 231
Whyte, W. F., 117
Woodward, J., 31, 147, 177, 212, 213

Zaleznik, A., 126, 132, 134, 140, 143, 214